IF YOU WERE GOD

THREE WORKS BY
ARYEH KAPLAN

IF YOU WERE GOD

IMMORTALITY AND THE SOUL

A WORLD OF LOVE

NCSY/ORTHODOX UNION

Published by the National Conference of
Synagogue Youth/Union of Orthodox Jewish
Congregations of America, 45 West 36th Street,
New York, NY 10018

Distributed in Israel by Mesorah Mafitzim/
J. Grossman, Rechov Bayit Vegan 90/5,
Jerusalem.

Produced by Olivestone Publishing Services
PRINTED IN THE UNITED STATES OF AMERICA

CONTENTS

IF YOU
WERE GOD

I form light and create darkness,
   I make peace and create evil,
   I am God, I do all these things....
Woe to the man who strives with his Maker...
   "What are you making?"
   or shall it say
   "Your work has no place?"
Woe to the man who says to his Father,
   "Why have you conceived me?"
   or to his mother
   "Why did you bear me?"....
Surely, You are a God Who hides,
   the God of Israel,
   the One Who saves.

Isaiah 45

I
The Problem

You ARE GIVEN an island where several tribes live.

By nature and culture, these tribes are exploitative and belligerent. This results in much suffering on the island, caused by war, poverty and prejudice.

They have been living this way for centuries without any sign of improvement.

YOUR ASSIGNMENT:

To try to improve this society.

To teach its members to live together in harmony and reduce suffering to a minimum or eliminate it entirely.

To create a healthy society.

YOUR RESOURCES:

You have all the resources that a highly advanced technology can offer.

You have the entire island under surveillance and can see what is happening in any place at any time.

You have such devices as cloud seeding equipment and can plant underground explosives. Within reason, you can control weather, flooding, volcanos and earthquakes, and produce any "natural" phenomenon on cue.

You also have devices that can be used to implant ideas through subliminal suggestion. You can implant ideas to entire populations or to certain select leaders.

However, you must take into account the severe limitations of subliminal suggestion. If you try to implant any ideas that go against the basic nature of the populace, they will be totally rejected and your efforts will be in vain.

One alternative would be to implant ideas that somehow would make use of the acknowledged bad nature of these people.

YOUR RESTRICTIONS:

Under no circumstances are the natives of this island to be aware of your presence.

This supersedes all other considerations.

The cultural shock caused by your revealing yourself would disrupt the entire fabric of the island culture. It would cause much suffering and more than offset any good that you could possibly accomplish.

The natives would be reduced to a state of almost vegetable-like dependence from which they would be unlikely to recover. If they did recover, they might rebel so violently as to eliminate any positive values they might have originally had.

Therefore, the restriction that you not reveal yourself must be followed *without exception under any circumstances.*

But aside from this restriction, you have a free hand to proceed as humanely or as ruthlessly as you see fit.

In short, you have the opportunity to play God.

What would you do?

II
The Questions

MANY PEOPLE SAY that these days it is very difficult to believe. We live in a generation that has seen the brutal murder of the six million. We have seen children burned to death in Vietnam, babies starved in Biafra, and a nation systematically decimated in Bangladesh. We see starvation, poverty and inequality wherever we look. Good people suffer and the dishonest seem to thrive.

Many people ask what seems to be a legitimate question: Why does God allow these things? Why doesn't He do something about it?

To some extent, the answer should be obvious. It is man, not God, who brings most evil to the world.[1] God does not make wars — men do. God did not kill the six million — men did. God does not oppress the poor — men do. God does not drop napalm — men do.

But people come back and argue that this does not really answer the question. The basic dilemma still remains: Why did God create the possibility of evil? Why does He allow it to exist at all?

To even begin to understand this, we must delve into the very purpose of creation.

This purpose requires a creature responsible for its own actions. This in turn requires that men have free will.

If God would have wanted a race of puppets, than He would have created puppets. If He would have wanted robots, then He would have made robots. But this is not what God wanted. He wanted human beings, with free will, responsible for their actions.

7

But as soon as you have free will, you have the possibility of evil. The deeper we probe, the clearer this becomes.

To the best of our understanding, God created the universe as an act of love.[2] It was an act of love so immense that the human mind cannot even begin to fathom it. God created the world basically as a vehicle upon which He could bestow His good.[3]

But God's love is so great that any good that He bestows must be the greatest good possible. Anything less would simply not be enough.

But what is the greatest good? What is the ultimate good that God can bestow on His creation?

If you think for a moment the answer should be obvious. The ultimate good is God Himself. The greatest good that He can bestow is Himself. There is no greater good than achieving a degree of unity with the Creator Himself. It is for this reason that God gave man the ability to resemble Himself.[4]

God therefore gave man free will.

Just as God acts as a free Being, so does man. Just as God operates without prior restraint, so does man. Just as God can do good as a matter of His own choice, so can man. According to many commentators, this is the meaning of man being created in the "image" of God.[5]

But if God's purpose does not permit man to be a robot, neither does it permit him to be a prisoner.

Just as man has free will, he must also have freedom of choice. A man locked up in prison may have the same free will as everybody else, but there is little that he can do with it. For man to resemble his Creator to the greatest possible extent, he must exist in an arena where he has a maximum freedom of choice. The more man resembles God in His omnipotence, the closer he can resemble Him in his free choice of the good.

To make this freedom of choice real, God also had to create the possibility of evil.[6] If nothing but good were possible, it would produce no benefit. To use the Talmudic metaphor, it would be like carrying a lamp in broad daylight.[7] The *Zohar* thus states, "The advantage of wisdom comes from darkness. If there were no darkness, then light would not be discernible, and would produce no benefit.... Thus, it is written (*Eccl. 7:14*), 'God has made one thing opposite the other.'"[8]

Just as God's purpose does not allow man to be a physical prisoner, neither does it permit him to exist in an intellectual prison. How would man behave if God were to constantly reveal Himself? Would he really be free? If man were constantly made aware that he was standing in the King's presence, could he go against His will? If God's existence were constantly apparent, this awareness would make man a prisoner.

This is one reason why God created a world which follows natural laws, and in this way conceals Himself.[9] Thus, our sages teach us, "The world follows its natural pattern, and the fools who do evil will eventually be judged."[10]

This is the concept of the Sabbath. After the initial act of creation, God withdrew, as it were, and allowed the world to operate according to laws of nature which He had created.[11] The "clock" had been made and wound up, and now could run with a minimum of interference. When we observe the Sabbath, we similarly refrain from interfering or making any permanent changes in the order of nature.[12]

But the questioner can probe still deeper. He can ask: Why did God allow so much evil to exist in man's nature to begin with? Why does it seem so natural for man to oppress his neighbor and make him suffer?

But here also, we must realize that man's arena of action is here in the physical world, and therefore he must be part of a universe where God's presence is eclipsed. The spiritual in man may soar in the highest transcendental realms, but man's body is essentially that of an animal.[13] Our sages teach us that man partakes of the essence of both angel and beast.[14] The *Zohar* goes a step further and tells us that in addition to the divine soul which separates man from lower forms of life, man also has an animal soul.[15]

When man first came into existence, there was a basic harmony existing between these two parts of his nature. His intellect and animal nature were able to exist together without any intrinsic conflict. He had the opportunity to live in harmony with nature, devoting all his energies to the spiritual.[16]

However, there was an element of temptation in this Garden of Eden. Man's destiny was to transcend his animal nature on a spiritual plane. But he also had the temptation to transcend it on a physical level, to partake of the Tree of Good and Evil.

Man succumbed to this temptation.

This Knowledge than came between the two basic elements in man, the animal and the human.[17] Man was no longer like the animal, bound to nature, in harmony with his basic nature. He still had all the desires, lusts and aggressive nature of the animal. But he also acquired the ability to use his intellect so that his animal nature would be directed against his fellow human beings. It is this conflict between his animal and human nature that thrusts man in the direction of evil. We are therefore taught that it is man's animal nature that is responsible for the *Yetzer HaRa, the evil in man*.[18]

But here again, God cannot be blamed.

The decision to partake of the Tree of Knowledge — to transcend his animal nature on a worldly plane — was a decision that man made as a matter of free choice.

As soon as man partook of the Tree of Knowledge, he *knew* good and evil. Morality became a matter of knowledge and conscious choice, rather than part of man's basic nature. He would now have to wrestle with a new nature, where the animal and angel in him are in conflict.

But we can probe still further. We can ask: Why could man not have been made better? Why did God not make him into something that was more angel and less animal?

Here too, the fault was man's. Our sages teach us that the prohibition against tasting the fruit of the Tree of Knowledge was only temporary. Man's spiritual nature was gradually developing in such a manner that he would have eventually been strong enough to master his animal instincts. When this time arrived, he could have partaken of the Tree of Knowledge without endangering his spiritual essence.[19]

Man was indeed destined to be more angel and less animal. However, this was now to be a gradual process. It was aborted by man's impatience, his partaking of Knowledge before its time. It was this Knowledge that brought him in conflict with his animal nature, and stunted his spiritual development, making the beast dominant.

This thread runs through the entire history of mankind. Man's knowledge gave him a technology that could create instruments of destruction, but his moral strength was not great enough to avoid misusing them. This has reached its peak in our generation, where man has the power to destroy his entire planet, either with nuclear weapons, or by poisoning his environment. Man's knowledge gives him tremendous power, but he still has not learned how to use this power for the good. This is the reason why the Messianic Age must soon arrive. Only then will man learn how to use his knowledge for the good.[20]

Until then, man is faced with this great dilemma. He has the knowledge to create great societies, but they always get out of control and degenerate. He can make great technological strides, but he does not have the moral strength to use them for good. One of the saddest comments on the human predicament is the fact that many of our greatest technological advancements have been made to further the cause of warfare.

Still, the basic question does not seem to go away. Admittedly, man has an evil nature and it is his own fault. But why doesn't God intervene? Why doesn't He open up the heavens and stop all this evil? Why didn't He send down a bolt of lightning and destroy the concentration camps? Why didn't He send down some kind of manna for the starving babies of Biafra and Bangladesh? Why didn't He stop the Napalm bombs from burning innocent Vietnamese children? Why doesn't He pull off a miracle and make all the world's nuclear bombs disappear? After all, He is God. He certainly can do it. So why doesn't He?

We are taught, however, that an overabundance of light does not rectify the vessels, but shatters them.[21]

What would happen to our society if miracles suddenly started taking place? How would we react to it?

Could we go about our daily affairs as if nothing had happened? Could the vast, complex structures, upon which our civilization rests, continue to exist if this direct awareness of God were suddenly thrust upon us?

Take a city like New York. It takes the efforts of tens of thousands to provide food and other necessities to such a huge city, and further thousands just to transport these needs. It takes another army to provide the city with water, electricity, heat, and the removal of waste. Could this structure survive the awareness of miracles? And if it did not, would not the suffering be all the greater? If God began a miraculous intervention, would He not have to do it all the way? Indeed, this might take place in the Messianic Age, but then, the time must be ripe.

How would we react to miracles? Probably very much in the same way primitive societies react to the "miracles" of those that are more advanced. The first reaction is one of shock, or what sociologists call cultural shock. The natives first lose interest in everything and become completely dependent on the more advanced culture. They cease to have a mind of their own and develop a lethargy where life grows devoid of meaning. The degeneration of the proud self-sufficient savage into the shifty, no account native is often as tragic as it is inevitable.

If a society is not completely destroyed by the initial cultural shock, it undergoes a second stage, that of rebellion. The primitive culture rebels against both the invaders and their values. This is why so many missionaries ended up in the proverbial cooking pot.

If man resembles an animal, then he resembles a wild animal rather than a domestic one.[22] It is man's destiny to be free, not subject to other men. Thus, the inevitable result of the introduction of a higher culture is to overwhelm a more primitive one.[23]

When a higher culture is introduced, the intial reaction of the natives is to become domesticated, to become like cattle or sheep. If the domestication is complete, the humanity of the native is obliterated, at least, until he assimilates the dominant culture. Otherwise, the natives rebel and reassert their natural humanity.

The same is essentially true of our relationship to God. As long as He is hidden, we can strive toward Him, and attain the Godly. But we do this as a matter of free choice and are not overwhelmed by it. But if God were to reveal Himself, the man would no longer be able to exist as a free entity. He would know that he was always under the scrutiny of his Master, and that would make him into something less than a man. He would become some kind of puppet or robot, with an essential ingredient of his humanness destroyed. The only alternative would be rebellion.

But either alternative could cause more evil and suffering than would be alleviated by God's original intervention. There would be too much light, and the vessels would be shattered.

There was only one time when God literally revealed Himself and visibly stepped in and changed the course of history. This was at the Exodus from Egypt, where He performed miracles both in Egypt and by the Red Sea. This episode was climaxed by the Revelation at Sinai, where an entire nation literally heard the voice of God.

What happened then?

The first reaction at Sinai was one of shock. The people simply could not endure the majesty of God's word, and our sages teach us that their souls literally left them.[24] Their reaction is expressed in the Biblical account of Sinai, where immediately afterward they told Moses (*Ex. 20:16*), "You speak to us and we will listen, but let not God speak with us any more, for we will die."

When the people overcame their initial shock, they proceeded to the second stage, that of rebellion. This took place just 40 days after the Revelation at Sinai. They went against God and all His teachings, reverting to idolatry and worshipping a golden calf. They had heard the Ten Commandments from God Himself just 40 days earlier, and now they were violating every one of them.

We learn a very important lesson from this. For God to reveal Himself to an unworthy vessel can do more harm than good. This is one important reason why God does not show His hand.

Many people say that they would believe if only they could witness some sign or miracle. Sinai showed us that even this is not enough if people do not want to believe.

From all this we can begin to understand one of the most basic restrictions that God imposes upon Himself. He is a hidden God, and does not reveal Himself. This is required by man's psychology as well as God's very purpose in creation. God only reveals Himself to such people whose faith is so great that the revelation makes no difference in his belief. As the Rambam (Maimonides) points out, the only major exception to this rule was the Exodus.[25]

III
The Solutions

TAKING INTO ACCOUNT God's most basic self-restrictions, we can now make some attempt to place ourselves in God's place.

Our most basic restriction is that we not reveal our hand.

Taking this restriction into account, we can return to our opening problem, and imagine a microcosm where we are in a position to play God.

This opening problem was discussed in a number of groups, and much of what follows is a result of their conclusions. However, before reading on, you might wish to re-read the problem, and attempt to draw your own conclusions.

Much of the discussion revolved around solutions involving something like a huge chess game with the entire island as the board. There would be moves and countermoves, with a strategy to attempt to maneuver the natives into a desired position. Like a chess grandmaster, you would attempt to keep control of the game at all times. Your "win" would be to achieve the desired result.

While you have enough resources to eventually win, certain problems immediately become apparent. Not the least is the fact that every move may take decades or even centuries. You might achieve results, but it is a very long, drawn out process. You might have all the time in the world, but each year brings all the more suffering.

There is an even more profound problem. Even more important

than influencing events is our ultimate goal of improving the values of
the natives. However, even though a lesson may be learned by one
generation, it may be equally forgotten by a succeeding generation. To
make positive values an integral part of the island's culture is a most
formidable task.

A constant thread of suggestion in these discussions involved
infiltration. We could try to influence the island through infiltrators.
As long as it was not obvious, it would be within the rules.

Such infiltration could serve two purposes. First of all, we could use
the infiltrators as an example. They could set up a model society, and if
it endured long enough, it might interest people in attempting to
emulate it or learn from it.

The infiltrators could also be used to teach the natives directly.
Gradually, parts of their culture could be introduced to the island, rais-
ing its moral level. This could rapidly accelerate the game's conclusion.

These infiltrators would always be in a position of great peril.
Operating on a different value system, they would always be considered outsiders. The more their message diverged from that of the majority, the more they would be resented. Scattered throughout the
island to spread their message, they would very likely become a persecuted minority. By the rules of the game, there would be very little you
could do to help them. At best, you would play your game in such a
way as to protect them as much as possible.

Because of the danger of revealing your hand, communication with
your infiltrators would have to be kept to a minimum. They would
have to live on this island for many generations, scattered among the
natives, and you would have to set up many safeguards to prevent
them from assimilating the corrupt values of the island. To some extent, their status as a persecuted minority may also help prevent such
assimilation. But essentially, they would have to play their role in ig-
norance of your overall strategy.

Gradually, the islanders would eventually become aware of your
presence. Once the game was ended, you might even be able to reveal
yourself. The infiltrators' role would also then be revealed. As part of
your organization, they would become the natural leaders and teachers of the island.

IV
The Conclusion

As YOU MIGHT have already guessed, examining this microcosm gives us considerable insight into the way that God interacts with the world. He is working to bring the world to a state of perfection, which in our tradition is the Messianic promise. It is a slow process, whereby God constantly manuevers the forces of history toward this end. This "game" is essentially all of human history.

You might have also recognized the infiltrators. They are the Jewish people, who were given the basis of a perfect society in the teachings of the Torah. A society living according to these God-given principles can set itself up as an example of a healthy society, free of all the social diseases of its surrounding culture.

When God first gave the Torah, He told the Jewish people (*Lev. 20:26*), "You shall be holy unto Me, for I, the Lord, am holy, and I have set you apart from the peoples, that you should be Mine."[26] It is Israel's mission to set such an example, as the Torah states (*Deut. 4:6*), "You must observe (these commandments) carefully and keep them, for they are your wisdom and understanding in the sight of the nations — when they hear of these statutes, they will say, 'Surely, this great nation is a wise and understanding people.'"

It is our task to bear witness to God's plan for humanity, as we find (*Isa. 43:10*), "You are My witnesses, says God, and My servant, whom I have chosen."[27] Likewise, God told His prophet (*ibid. 42:6*), "I, the

16

Lord, have called you in righteousness...and have set you for a covenant of the people, for a light unto the nations."[28]

We are thus taught that Israel is like the heart of humanity, constantly beating and infusing all mankind with faith in God and His teachings.[29]

It was in this spirit that Judaism gave birth to both Christianity and Islam. Although far from perfection, these religions are a step in the right direction away from paganism.[30] The final step is yet to be made.

More important, however, is the fact that the Jewish people, at least those who keep the Torah, continue to stand as an example of a perfect society designed by God. The Torah and its commandments indeed represent the highest wisdom in perfecting human society. The Tzaddik is the closest that we can come to the perfect human being.

Israel's unique position in accepting God's Torah will eventually result in the destruction of all competing cultures. It would also temporarily result in Israel's earning the hatred of these cultures.[31] Our sages teach us that just as an olive must be crushed before it brings forth its oil, so is Israel often persecuted before its light shines forth.[32] Thus, God told His prophet (*Isa. 42:3,4*), "A bruised reed, he shall not break, a dimly burning wick, he shall not be extinguished, he shall make justice shine forth in truth. He shall not fail nor be crushed, until he has right in the earth, and the islands shall await the teachings of his Torah."[33]

We live in an age of many questions. The newspapers and television bring the horrors of the world onto our front doorstep and into our living rooms. What was once hidden by the barrier of intercontinental distance is now before our very eyes. We see the suffering and killling and starvation, and ask how God can tolerate such evil. For the Jew, the question of the six million always looms in the foreground of any such discussion.

But for one who understands the true depths of Judaism, there is no question. When you have probed into the very reason for existence and purpose of creation, not only do you find answers, but the questions themselves cease to exist.

One of the great Jewish leaders of today is the Klausenberger

Rebbe. He lost his wife, children and family to the Nazis, and himself spent two years in the hell of Auschwitz. Yet, he emerged from all this to rally a generation of concentration camp refugees back to Judaism, found a community in Williamsburg, and eventually build a settlement in Israel.

I often heard this great leader discuss the concentration camps and the six million. There are tears and sadness, but no questions. For here we have a Tzadik, whose great mind can see beyond the immediate. When one's gaze is on the Ultimate, there truly are no questions.

The most important thing to remember is that God is the ultimate good, and therefore, even the worst evil will eventually revert to good.[34] Man may do evil, but even this will be redeemed by God and ultimately be turned into good. The Talmud teaches us that in this world we must bless God for both good and evil, but in the Future World, we will realize that there is nothing but good.[35]

Notes

1. *Moreh Nevuchim* 3:10.
2. Cf. *Magid Devarab LeYaakov* #102, *Likutey Moharan* #64.
3. *Emunos VeDeyos* 1:4 end, 3:0, *Or HaShem* (Crescas) 2:6:2, *Sefer HaYashar* 1, *Pardes Rimonim* 2:6, *Sheur Kuma* (RaMaK) 13:3, *Etz Chaim, Shaar HaKellalim* #1, *Reshis Chochmah, Shaar HaT'shuvah* #1, *Shnei Luchos HaBris, Bais Yisroel* (Jerusalem 5720) 1:21b, *Shomrei Emunim (HaKadmon)* 2:13, *Mesilas Yesharim* #1, *Derech HaShem* 1:2:1.
4. *Derech HaShem, ibid.*
5. Cf. *Mechilta* on Ex. 14:29, *Bereshis Rabbah* 21:5, *Shir HaShirim Rabbah* 1:46, *Yad, Tshuvah* 5:1.
6. Cf. *Midrash Tehillim* 36:4, *Zohar* 1:23a, 2:184a, *Akedas Yitzchok* 70 (3:145b), *Etz Chaim, Shaar HaMelachim* 5, *Sefer Baal Shem Tov, Sh'mos* #9.
7. *Chulin* 60b.
8. *Zohar* 3:47b.
9. *Bereshis Rabbah* 9:6, *Menoras HaMaor* 237, *Tosefos Yom Tov* on *Avodah Zara* 4:7, Cf. *Ikkarim* 4:12 on Eccl. 8:11.
10. *Avodah Zarah* 54b.
11. *Moreh Nevuchim* 2:28 on Ps. 148:6. Cf. *Zohar* 1:138b, *Berachos* 60b. Also see Rashi, Ibn Ezra, Sforno on Eccl. 3:14.
12. *Shabbos* 12:1 (102b).
13. *Sifri, Haazinu* 306, *Bereshis Rabbah* 8:11, Rashi in Gen. 2:7.
14. *Chagigah* 16a.
15. *Zohar* 2:94b.
16. Cf. Ramban on Gen. 2:9; *Kiddushin* 4:14 (82a).
17. *Kisvey HaAri: Shemonah Shaarim, Shaar HaPesukim* on Gen.2:17, *Likutey Torah* (HaAri) on Gen. 3:1.
18. *Etz Chaim, Shaar Kitzur ABYA* #3 ff; *Shaarey Kedusha* #1, *Likutey Amarim (Tanya)* #1.
19. *Toras Moshe (Chasam Sofer)* on Gen. 2:17, *Tosefos, Sanhedrin* 56b "Lo." See note 17.

20. See note 17. Also see Bechaya on Gen. 2:9; *Derech HaShem* 1:3.
21. *Etz Chaim, Shaar HaMelachim* 5.
22. See *Kelayim* 8:5, where the *Adney HaSadeh* is found to have an affinity to both a wild animal (*Chayah*) and man. *Meleches Shlema ibid.* 8:6.
23. *Zohar* 1:24b, Maharal, *Beer HaGolah* (Pardes, Tel Aviv) p. 39b. Cf. *Shabbos* 89b, *Sh'mos Rabbah* 2:6.
24. *Zohar* 2:84b.
25. Moreh Nevuchim 2:35, from Deut. 34.1.
26. See Rashi *ad loc.* Cf. Lev. 19:2.
27. Mahari Kara *ad loc., Ikkarim* 1:2. Cf. Isa 43:21, 44:8.
28. This is part of the famous "suffering servant" passage in Isaiah. According to Rashi and the Mahari Kara, this is speaking of Israel. See *Midrash Tehillim* 2:9. However, others, such as the Targum, Radak and Metzudos, state that it refers to the Messiah. See *Midrash Tehillim* 43:1. Ibn Ezra, on the other hand, states that it refers to the prophet himself. For further discussion, see Abarbanel *ad loc.*
29. *Zohar* 2:221b, *Kuzari* 3:36 (51b), 2:12 (13a).
30. *Kuzari* 4:23, *Tshuvos Rambam* 58, *Tshuvos Rivash* 119, *Akedas Yitzchok* 88.
31. See note 23.
32. *Sh'mos Rabbah* 36:1.
33. See note 28. Cf. *Menachos* 53b.
34. Rabbi Moshe Chaim Luzatto, *KaLaCh Pis'chey Chochmah* #2.
35. *Pesachim* 50a.

IMMORTALITY
AND THE SOUL

I
Meet the Real You

LOOK AT YOUR hand. What do you see?

A part of your body, an appendage made of bone and sinew covered with flesh and skin. It is filled with nerves, blood vessels and lymph ducts which run through it and connect it to your body, making it part of you.

You can open and close your hand. It obeys every command that your mind sends to it. It is yours—a part of you. But what are you? Who is the real you? What happens when you tell your hand to open and close? How does your mind will it to obey its commands?

Now point a finger at yourself. If you are an average person, you will point a finger at your chest. You think of yourself as your body. But is your body the real you?

Not too long ago, a person could consider his own body an integral part of himself. You were your body and your body was you. But this is no longer the case. Scientific progress has changed the entire concept of human personality and identity.

Heart transplants are now an almost commonplace occurrence. They do not even make the news any more. A man can live with another person's heart beating in his breast. If we would ask such a man to point to himself, would he point at his heart? Is this transplanted heart really part of him? Is the heart that beats within your breast the real you? Or is it something else entirely?

Researchers are predicting that within the next decade or two, brain transplants may be possible. This would force us to completely re-evaluate the concept of human personality.

Imagine what it would be like to undergo a brain transplant. A man might be suffering from an incurable disease in his body, but still have a healthy brain. The donor, on the other hand, would have suffered ir-reparable brain damage, but otherwise have a perfectly sound body. The brain is removed from the sick body and placed in the healthy one.

Who is the new man? We have an old brain with all its memories, personality traits and behavior patterns. But it has a brand new body. The old body might have been old and sick, while the new one may be young and full of energy.

Let us ask this man to point to himself. Will he point to his body? Is the real you your body or your brain?

(Actually, an analogous question is raised in the Talmud. As is well known, in the case of an unsolved murder, a special sacrifice, the *Eglah Arufah*, was brought by the city nearest the corpse.[1] The Mishnah raises two questions. What if the head is found in one place and the body in another?[2] And if the body is equidistant from the two cities, from what portion of the body do we measure?[3] In both cases, Rabbi Eliezer states that we measure from the body, while Rabbi Akiba states that we measure from the head. The *Halachah* follows Rabbi Akiba.[4])

A brain transplant raises enough questions. How about a memory transfer?

The science of cybernetics has discovered many similarities between computers and the human brain. Computer technology allows one to program a memory transfer, taking all the information contained in one computer and transferring it to another. All that passes from one computer to the other is information.

What if this were done with the human brain? This may lie in the realm of science fiction, but even if it will never be possible in practice, it is certainly possible in theory.

Let us try to envision such a memory transfer. Assume we have a person with an incurable disease where neither the body nor the brain can be salvaged. We clone a new body for this individual, brain and all. The possibilities of doing this have already been discussed at length in the literature. This new body has a blank new brain, capable of functioning, but without any memories or thought patterns. As a final step, we accomplish a memory transfer, bringing all the information from the sick person into the brain of the new body.

We now have a fascinating situation. If all of a man's memories, thought patterns and personality traits are transferred to a new body and brain, this person literally exists in his new body. But nothing physical has been transferred. No physical part of him has been placed in the new body. All that has been placed in this new body is information that previously existed in the old brain. Yet this information contains the sum total of this person's personality.

But if this is true, then it offers us tremendous new insight into our original question: Who is the real you?

The real you is not your body or brain, but the information contained in your brain — your memories, personality traits and thought patterns.

(The philosophical Kabbalists write that the spiritual world is a realm whose substance is information. It is an arena where information can interact without being attached to or dependent on matter. Thus, an angel, for example, can interact with another angel, even though they have no connection with anything material. Angels can also interact with material objects. Such a spiritual world would also be able to interact with the information comprising the human persona.)

What happens then when a person dies?

We know that the body ceases to function. The brain becomes inert and the physical man is dead.

But what happens to the real you — the human personality? What happens to all this information — the memories, thought patterns and personality traits? When a book is burned its contents are no longer available. When a computer is smashed, the information within it is also destroyed. Does the same thing happen when a man dies? Is the mind and personality irretrievably lost?

We know that God is omniscient. He knows all and does not forget. God knows every thought and memory that exists within our brains. There is no bit of information that escapes His knowledge.

What, then, happens when a man dies? God does not forget, and therefore all of this information continues to exist, at least in God's memory.

(An allusion to this is also found in the Kaballah. *Gan Eden* or *Paradise* is said to exist in the *sephirah* of *Binah* — the divine understanding.[5] This may well be related to the concept of memory. Souls, on the other hand, are conceived in the *sephirah* of *Daas* — knowledge.[6] One may say that while we live, we exist in God's knowledge (*Daas*), while after death we exist in His memory (*Binah*).)

We may think of something existing only in memory as being static and effectively dead. But God's memory is not a static thing. The sum total of a human personality may indeed exist in God's memory, but it can still maintain its self-identity and volition, and remain in an active state.

This sum total of the human personality existing in God's memory is what lives on even after a man dies.

(This may well be why the Kabbalists speak of this as *Binah* — understanding, rather than memory. For understanding is a dynamic process, where information contained in one's memory interacts in an active manner. The soul is not in a passive memory state, but in a dynamic state of *Binah*.)

The concept of immortality and of the soul may well be outside the realm of human comprehension. "No eye has seen it other than God." However, our limited understanding of both God and man can provide us with some degree of perception into our ultimate future.

(In a Kabbalistic sense, we are here speaking about the lowest level of the soul, the *Nefesh HaBehemis* or "animal soul."[7] This most probably can be identified with the information contained in the human brain. However, this interacts with the higher parts of the soul, *Nefesh, Ruach* and *Neshamah*.)

To speak of a concept such as God's memory is indeed very difficult. It involves a deep discussion of the entire transcendental sphere. We therefore give it names that have meaning to us, such as *Gan Eden*, Paradise, the World to Come, the World of Souls,[8] or the bond of eternal life. However, the Bible speaks of immortality as a return to God Himself (*Eccl. 12:7*): "The dust returns to the dust as it were, but the spirit returns to God Who gave it."

II
Naked Before God

WE HAVE SEEN that our knowledge of the mind and our traditions regarding God can give us some handle on the question of immortality.

But what is immortality like? What is it like to be a disembodied soul? How does it feel to be in the World of Soul?

We know that the human brain, marvelous organ that it is, is still very inefficient as a thinking device. Henri Bergson has suggested that one of the main functions of the brain and nervous system is to eliminate activity and awareness, rather than produce it.

Aldous Huxley[9] quotes Prof. C.D. Broad's comments on this. He says that every person is capable of remembering everything that has ever happened to him. He is able to perceive everything that surrounds him. However, if all this information poured into our minds at once, it would overwhelm us. So the function of the brain and nervous system is to protect us and prevent us from being overwhelmed and confused by the vast amount of information that impinges upon our sense organs. They shut out most of what we perceive and remember. All that would confound us is eliminated and only the small, special selection that is useful is allowed to remain.

Huxley explains that our mind has powers of perception and concentration that we cannot even begin to imagine. But our main business is to survive at all costs. To make survival possible, all of our mind's capabilities must be funneled through the reducing valve of the brain.

Some researchers are studying this effect. They believe that this reducing-valve effect may be very similar to the jamming equipment used to block out offensive radio broadcasts. The brain constantly produces a kind of static, cutting down our perception and reducing our mental activity.

This static can actually be seen. When you close your eyes, you see all sorts of random pictures flashing through your mind. It is impossible to concentrate on any one of them for more than an instant, and each image is obscured by a host of others superimposed over it.

This static can even be seen when your eyes are opened. However, one usually ignores these images since they are so faint compared to our visual perception. However, they still reduce one's perception, both of the world around him and of himself.

Much of what we know about this static is a result of research done with drugs that eliminate it. According to a number of authorities, this is precisely how the psychedelic drugs work.

Now imagine the mental activity of a disembodied soul, standing naked before God. The reducing valve is gone entirely. The mind is open and transparent. Things can be perceived in a way that is impossible to a mind held back by a body and nervous system. The visions and understanding are the most delightful bliss imaginable (as per: "the righteous, sitting with their crowns on their heads, delighting in the shine of the *Shechinah*."[10])

This is what Job meant when he said (19:26), "And when after my skin is destroyed, then without my flesh shall I see God."

But then, an individual will also see himself in a new light. Every thought and memory will be lucid, and he will see himself for the first time without the static and jamming that shuts out most thoughts.

Even in our mortal physical state, looking at oneself can sometimes be pleasing and at other times very painful. Certain acts leave us proud and pleased with ourselves. Others cause excruciating pains, especially when we are caught.

Imagine standing naked before God, with your memory wide open, completely transparent without any jamming mechanism or reducing valve to diminish its force. You will remember everything you ever did and see it in a new light. You will see it in the light of the unshaded spirit, or, if you will, in God's own light that shines from one end of creation to the other. The memory of every good deed and *Mitzvah* will be the sublimest of pleasures, as our tradition speaks of *Olam Haba.*

But your memory will also be open to all the things of which you are ashamed. They cannot be rationalized away or dismissed. You will be facing yourself, fully aware of the consequences of all your deeds. We all know the terrible shame and humiliation experienced when one is caught in the act of doing something wrong. Imagine being caught by one's own memory with no place to escape. This indeed, may be what Daniel is alluding to when he says (*Dan. 12:2*), "And many of them that sleep in the dust shall awake, some to everlasting life, and some to reproach and everlasting shame."

A number of our great teachers[11] write that the fire of *Gehenom* is actually the burning shame one experiences because of his sins. Again, this may be alluded to in the words of the prophet (*Isa. 66:24*), "And they shall go forth and look upon the carcasses of the men that have rebelled against Me; for their worm shall not die, nor shall their fire be quenched, and they shall be ashamed before all flesh." We find that evil leads to shame, as it is written (*Jer. 7:19*), "Are they angering Me, says God, are they not provoking themselves, to their own shame... Behold My anger...shall not burn, and shall not be quenched." The main concept of reward is that it be without shame, as we find (*Joel 2:26*), "And you shall eat and be satisfied...and my people shall never be ashamed."

The Talmud provides us with even stronger evidence that shame burns like fire. It states, "Rabbi Chanana says; this teaches us that each one (in the World of Souls) is burned by the canopy of his companion. Woe, for that shame! Woe, for that humiliation."[12] We find that shame is a major form of punishment in the Midrash on the verse (*Ps. 6:11*), "All your enemies shall be ashamed and very confounded:" Rabbi Joshua ben Levi says, "God only curses the wicked with shame."[13] This is also alluded to in the Talmudic statement, "It is better for Amram to suffer shame in this world, and not in the World to come."[14] Similarly, "Blessed is God who gave him shame in this world and not the next."[15] When the *Zohar* speaks of the future reward, it says, "Happy is he who comes here without shame."[16]

Of course, these concepts of fire and shame, as used by our Sages, may also contain deeper mysteries and meanings. But taken literally, one says that a major ingredient of fire may be shame.[17] How else could one characaterize the agony of unconcealed shame upon a soul?

We are taught that the judgment of the wicked lasts 12 months.[18] Even the naked soul can gradually learn to live with this shame and forget it, and the pain eventually subsides. It may be more than coincidence that 12 months is also the length of time required for something to be forgotten in Talmudic law. Thus, one mourns a parent for 12 months,[19] and says a special blessing upon seeing a close friend after this period of time.[20] (Of course, there is an exception to this rule. There are the nonbelievers and worst of sinners reckoned in the Talmud.[21] These individuals have nothing else but their shame and have no escape from everlasting torment.)

But even temporary torment is beyond our imagination. The Ramban (Nachmanides) writes that all the suffering of Job would not compare to an instant in *Gehenom*.[22] Rabbi Nachman of Breslov says the same of a man who suffered for years from the most indescribable torments: it is still better than a single burn in *Gehenom*.[23] Mental torture cannot be compared to the mere physical.

Here again, when we speak of *Gan Eden* and *Gehenom*, we find that we are not discussing mystical concepts, but ideas that are well within the realm of scientific psychology, such as shame. We can now proceed a step further.

III
What the Dead Think of Us

THERE IS ANOTHER dimension of immortality discussed in the Talmud. It asks: Do the dead know what is happening in the world of the living?[24]

After an involved discussion, the Talmud concludes that they do have this awareness.[25] The Kaballistic philosophers explain that the soul achieves a degree of unity with God, the source of all knowledge, and therefore also partakes of His omniscience.

When a man dies, he enters a new world of awareness. He exists as a disembodied soul and yet is aware of what is happening in the physical world. Gradually, he learns to focus on any physical event he wishes. At first this is a frightening experience. You know that you are dead. You can see your body lying there, with your friends and relatives standing around crying over you. We are taught that immediately after death, the soul is in a great state of confusion.[26]

What is the main source of its attention? What draws its focus more than anything else?

We are taught that it is the body. Most people identify themselves with their bodies, as we have discussed earlier. It is difficult for a soul to break this thought habit, and therefore, for the first few days, the soul is literally obsessed with its previous body. This is alluded to in the verse (*Job 14:22*), "And his soul mourns for him."[27]

This is especially true before the body is buried.[28] The soul wonders what will happen to the body. It finds it to be both fascinating and frightening to watch its own body's funeral arrangements and preparation for burial.

Of course, this is one of the reasons why Judaism teaches us that we must have the utmost respect for human remains. We can imagine how painful it is for a soul to see its recent body cast around like an animal carcass. The Torah therefore forbids this.

This is also related to the question of autopsies. We can imagine how a soul would feel when seeing its body lying on the autopsy table, being dissected and examined.

The disembodied soul spends much of its time learning how to focus. It is now seeing without physical eyes, using some process which we do not even have the vocabulary to describe. The Kabbalists call this frightening process *Kaf HaKela*—it is like being thrown with a sling from one end of the world to another.[29] It is alluded to in the verse (*1 Sam. 25:29*), "The soul of my master shall be bound up in the bundle of life with the Lord your God, and the souls of your enemies shall He sling out, as from the hollow of a sling." The soul perceives things flashing into focus from all over, and is in a state of total confusion and disorientation.

One of the few things that the soul has little difficulty focusing on is its own body. It is a familiar pattern and some tie seems to remain. To some extent, it is a refuge from its disorientation.

Of course the body begins to decompose soon after it is buried. The effect of watching this must be both frightening and painful. The Talmud teaches us, "Worms are as painful to the dead as needles in the flesh of the living, as it is written (*Job 14:22*), 'his flesh grieves for him.'"[30] Most commentaries write that this refers to the psychological anguish of the soul in seeing its earthly habitation in a state of decay.[31] The Kabbalists call this *Chibut Ha Kever*,[32] the punishment of the grave. We are taught that what happens to the body in the grave can be an even worse experience than *Gehenom*.[33]

This varies among individuals. The more one is obsessed with one's body and the material world in general during his lifetime, the more he will be obsessed with it after death. For the man to whom the material was everything, this deterioration of the body is most painful. On the other extreme, the person who was immersed in the spiritual, may not care very much about the fate of his body at all. He finds himself very much at home in the spiritual realm and might quickly forget about his body entirely. This is what we are taught. Tzadikim are not bothered by *Chibut HaKever* at all, since they never consider their worldly body overly important.[34]

In general, adjustment to the spiritual world depends greatly on one's preparation in this world. Our traditions teach us that the main preparation is through Torah.

Many of us think of death as a most frightening experience. Tzadikim, on the other hand, have looked forward to it. Shortly before his death, Rabbi Nachman Bretslaver said, "I very much want to divest myself of this garment that is my body."[35] If we truly believe and trust in a merciful God, then death has no terror for us.

This is a description of what our tradition teaches us about the soul's existence. Most of these facts are from the teachings of *Chazal* in the Talmud and Midrash as interpreted by the Kaballists. Here we have synthesized their interpretations with the terminology of modern scientific concepts. The result is a consistent view of soul and human personality as realities which do not possess the body's temporal discontinuity called "death."

Notes

1. Deut. 21:1–9.
2. *Sotah* 9:3 (45b).
3. *Ibid.* 9:4.
4. *Yad Chazakah, Rotzeach* 9:9.
5. *Shaarey Orah* 8; *Pardes Rimonim* 8:9, 23:3.
6. *Etz Chaim, Shaar MaN U'MaD* 4, *Shaar HaKlipos* 2.
7. Cf. *Zohar* 2:94b.
8. See *Derech HaShem* 1:3:11.
9. Aldous Huxley, *The Doors of Perception* (Harper & Row, N.Y. 1970) p. 22 f.
10. *Berachos* 17a.
11. *Ikkarim* 4:33, *Nishamas Chaim* 1:13.
12. *Baba Basra* 75a.
13. *Midrash Tehilim a. l.*
14. *Kiddushin* 81a.
15. *Yebamos* 105b.
16. *Zohar* 1:4a.
17. *Toras HaAdam, Shaar HaGemul* (Jerusalem, 5715) p. 78a.
18. *Eduyos* 2:10.
19. *Moed Katan* 22b.
20. *Berachos* 58b.
21. *Rosh HaShanah* 17a.
22. *Ramban,* introduction to Job.
23. *Sichos HaRan* 235.
24. *Berachos* 18b.
25. See *Tosfos, Shabbos* 153a *"VeNishmaso," Sotah* 34b *"Avoi" Maaver Yavek* 2:25, *Nishmas Chaim* 2:22.
26. *Taz, Yoreh Deah* 339:3. Cf. *Avodah Zara* 20b, *Pirkei Rabbi Eliezer.*
27. *Shabbos* 152a, *Midrash Ne'elam, Zohar* 1:122b.
28. *Shabbos* 152b, *Sefer Mitzvos Gadol, Esin DeRabanan* 2 (Vinitzia, 5307) p. 246a.

29. *Shabbos, ibid., Maharsha a. l., Zohar* 1:217b, 3:185b, 222b.
30. *Berachos* 18b, *Shabbos* 152a.
31. *Emunos VeDeyos* 6:7, *Tshuvos Rashba* 369, *Sefer Chasidim* 1163, *Tosfos Yom Tov* 2:7, *Tshuvos Sh'vus Yaakov* 2:97, Zvi Hirsh Chayos on *Shabbos* 13b. Cf. *Tanchuma, VaYikra* 8.
32. *Emunos VeDeyos, ibid, Nishmas Chaim* 2:24, *Maaver Yavak* 2:7.
33. *Midrash Chibut HaKever* in *Reshis Chochmah, Shaar HaYirah* 12, #3.
34. *Emunos VeDeyos, ibid.* Cf. *Midrash Ne'elam, Zolar* 1:123a.
35. *Sichos HaRan* 179.

A WORLD OF LOVE

The Purpose of Creation

I

Why did God create the world?

The question is both very simple, and yet, at the same time involves some of the most sublime mysteries. For the truth is that we do not have the power to understand God, and just as we cannot understand Him, so can we not understand His reasons. But if we cannot understand God, we can try to understand the world, and ask why it exists. We can look and see what God Himself has taught us about the purpose of creation, both in the Bible and in our traditions.

As our sages teach us, there is absolutely nothing positive that we can say about God Himself. He exists — and we can say no more. But we can speak of His relationship with His world.

One of the main things that we can say about God in this manner is that He is good. Not only do we say that God *is* good, but also that He defines good. Every act of God contains the most pure and infinite Good that can exist. His goodness and love are the two most basic of God's qualities as far as we can understand, and they work together to bring about His purpose. The Psalmist sings of this and says (*Psalm 145:9*), "God is good to all, His love rests on all His deeds."[1]

God had absolutely no need to create the world. God Himself is absolute perfection, and has no need for anything, even creation. When He created the world, He therefore performed the most perfect possible act of altruism and love. No matter how selfless a human act may be, there is always some benefit to the doer, even if it is nothing more than a degree of self-satisfaction. But God, on the other hand, has no needs or wants, and therefore, there was nothing about Him that creation could satisfy. It was therefore the most perfect possible act of love. The Psalmist again speaks of this and says (*Psalm 89:1*), "I have said: 'The world is built of love.'"[2]

We say that God is good because He acts in love. Neither His good nor His love are in any way limited. There is an often repeated chant that speaks of both God's goodness and His love. It goes (*Psalm 136:1*), "Give thanks to God, His love is infinite."[3]

God was under absolutely no compulsion to create the world.[4] We therefore call His creation an act of pure and infinite love. The litany thus continues (*ibid. 136:5–9*):

He made the heavens with wisdom	His love is infinite.
Set the earth on the waters	His love is infinite.
He makes the great lights	His love is infinite.
The sun to rule the day	His love is infinite.
The moon and stars by night	His love is infinite.

The Baal Shem Tov explains this in a somewhat deeper manner.[5] We know that God knows the future just as He knows the past. Therefore, even before creation, God knew of mankind. And just as He knew man, He loved man. It was this love of generations yet unborn that brought God to create the universe. God saw the good people of every generation, and His love for them served as a focus for creation. Our sages thus teach us that God perceived the deeds of the righteous before creating the world.[6] He therefore told us through His prophet (*Jeremiah 31:3*), "With an infinite world of love have I loved you, therefore, I have drawn you to Me with affection."

God Himself calls His creation an act of goodness. It is for this reason that at the end of creation the Torah says (*Genesis 1:35*), "And God saw all that He had made, and behold, it was very good."[7] What God is telling us in the Torah is that creation is an expression of His good.

The Talmud tells us a story that expresses this most graphically:[8]

Rabbi Akiba was once travelling. With him, he had a donkey, a rooster, and a torch. He came to a city and sought lodging, but they would not let him stay for the night. Rabbi Akiba did not complain. He merely remarked, "All that God does is for the good."

Having no other choice, he camped in a field. During the night, a lion came and killed his donkey. Later, a cat came and ate his rooster. Finally, a wind came and extinguished his torch. Again, he said, "All that God does is for the good."

In the morning, Rabbi Akiba walked back to the city where he had sought to spend the night. He found the city sacked and all its inhabitants killed. If he would have spent the night there, he would have been among the dead. If the Romans would have heard his donkey bray, or his rooster crow, or if they would have seen his torch, they would have found him and killed him. Realizing all this, he exclaimed, "Have I not said that all God does is for the good."

What Rabbi Akiba is teaching us is that everything that God does is ultimately good. There are things that may seem to contradict this. There are things that may seem to be bad and evil. But ultimately, everything comes from good and will end up as good.[9] If we have the patience, we will see that everything in the world is ultimately good.

Everything in creation is part of God's plan. God's plan is the ultimate good. The wise Solomon thus teaches us (*Proverbs 16:4*), "God made everything for His purpose, even the wicked for the day of evil." The Talmud comments on this, saying, "Everything that God created in His world, He created for His glory."[10]

Of course, there is a limit beyond which we cannot ask. We cannot ultimately understand God's motive in creation, any more than we can understand anything else about His being. Ultimately, He created for His own purpose, unknown to any being other than Himself. The final statement that we must make is that God created the world for His own reasons, or in His word to His prophet (*Isaiah 43:7*), "Everything that is called by My name, for My glory, I created, formed and made it."[11] When God speaks of His glory, He means that it was for Himself—for His own reason, beyond all human comprehension.[12] With relation to ourselves, we call God's motives "good." But in relation to God Himself, it is totally beyond our understanding.[13]

But God had a plan for the world, and this plan was ultimate Good. The expression of this plan was the Torah, and as such, it served as the blueprint for all creation.[14] Thus, God Himself calls the Torah good, as He told the wise Solomon (*Proverbs 4:2*), "I have given you a good thing, do not forsake My Torah." Our sages explain that this means that the Torah is God's ultimate plan of good for the world, and say, "There is no good other than Torah."[15]

It was this plan that ultimately led God to create the world. Good cannot be given unless there is someone to receive it. There is a Midrash that expresses this quite clearly, teaching us that God asked the Torah if He should create the universe. The Torah replied, "If the King has no camp, then over what is He a King?"[16]

What this Midrash is teaching us is that once God had created the Torah, then it could tell Him to create a world. This means that once God had made His plan to do good, then He had to make a world to receive it. In a sense, we can say that God was drawn to create the world by His own plan.[17] The plan itself could "tell" God, "There is no King without a kingdom," as the scripture itself echoes (*Proverbs 14:8*), "In a multitude of people is a King's glory."[18]

II

WE SAY THAT God created the world in order to bestow good to it. But what is this good? What good does God have to offer His world?

First of all, we must realize that any good that God gives must be the ultimate good that His creation can accept. The Psalmist said (*Psalm 31:20*), "How great is Your good, stored up for those who fear You." Our sages interpret this to say that God bestows good in the greatest possible abundance.[19] In another place, they teach us that this verse means that God is telling us, "You according to your strength, and Me according to Mine."[20] In other words, God gives us the greatest good that we can possibly accept.

But what is this ultimate good? What is the greatest possible good that God can bestow?

If we think about it, the answer is really quite simple. The greatest possible good is God Himself.[21] There is no other ultimate true good. The Psalmist thus said (*Psalm 16:2*), "I have no good but You." In the Talmud, Rabbi Acha interprets this to mean that no true good exists in the world, except that of God Himself.[24]

The ultimate good is therefore to partake of God, and it is this good that He planned to give the world. He would create a world where creatures ultimately could partake of His essence. The Psalmist sings of this (*Psalm 34:9*), "Taste and see that God is good, happy is the man who finds refuge in Him."

God therefore created the world in such a way that man could draw close to Him and partake of His essence. Of course, we are not speaking of physical closeness, but of spiritual closeness. Such closeness involves the knowledge and understanding of God, as well as resembling Him to the greatest degree possible. We will later discuss how these two concepts are related, but ultimately, both are spiritual closeness.

Here again, we hear this in the words of the Psalmist (*Psalm 73:28*), "But for me, the nearness of God is good. I have made God my refuge, that I may tell of His works." The Psalmist is teaching us that his ultimate good is nearness to God. This nearness involves "telling of His works" — that is, a deep knowledge and perception of the Divine.[25]

The ultimate good that God offers is therefore the opportunity to perceive Him. In one place, our sages thus teach us that God created the world in order that men may know Him.[26] This is not a separate reason, but the way in which He bestows His good upon us.[27] God thus told us through His prophet (*Isaiah 48:17*), "I am your God, I teach you for your good." The Psalmist expresses the same idea when he says (*Psalm 119:68*), "You are good and You do good: teach me Your statutes."

To know God and understand Him in any way is to have a deep awe and dread of His majesty. All true wisdom is that of God. But such wisdom and knowledge imply the fear and reverence of God. The Psalmist thus said (*Psalm 111:10*), "The beginning of wisdom is the fear of God." The wise Solomon expresses the same idea when he says (*Proverbs 1:7*), "The fear of God is the beginning of knowledge."[28]

We can therefore say that the ultimate goal of creation is that we should come close to God, and therefore both know and fear Him. Again we hear the words of Solomon (*Ecclesiastes 3:14*), "Whatever God does shall be forever...God has made it so that man should fear Him." The Talmud comments on this, saying that the world was created for the fear of God.[29] This is man's true purpose in the world, as again we find (*ibid.12:13*), "The sum of the matter, when all has been heard: Fear God and keep His commandments, for this is all of man." In the Talmud, Rabbi Eleazar comments on this and says, "Solomon is teaching us that all the world was created for the fear of God."[30]

When our sages say that the world was created for the fear of God, they are not contradicting the teaching that it was created as a vehicle for His good. What they are doing is expressing what this good ultimately is. It is a knowledge of God that is most perfectly expressed by the reverence and awe that we call the "fear of God."

The ultimate place where we will be worthy of this vision and perception will be in what we call *Olam HaBah* — the Future World or the World to Come. It is a world of absolute life and goodness. It is of the vision of the World to Come that the Psalmist is speaking of when he says (*Psalm 27:13*), "I believe that I will gaze upon God in the land of the living." This "land of the living" is the Future World.[31]

It is this future world that is the goal of all creation. Our sages thus teach us, "This world is like an antechamber before the World to Come. Prepare yourself in the antechamber before you enter the palace."[32]

Since this Future World is the ultimate goal of creation, it is also the place of ultimate good. In the language of the Talmud, it is called, "the World where all is good."[33] It is a good that surpasses anything that this world may possibly have to offer. This is what our sages mean when they say, "One moment of delight in the Future World is more than all the good of this world."[34]

We can obtain some idea of what this Future World will be like from a common saying of Rav, quoted in the Talmud.[35] He said, "In the Future World, there will be no eating, drinking, childbearing or business. Neither will there be jealousy, hatred or strife. The righteous will sit with their crowns on thieir heads, delighting in the radiance of the Divine Presence."

Our sages teach us that this "radiance of the Divine Presence" is a perception of the Divine.[36] In the Future World, we will perceive and comprehend God in the greatest degree possible.

This perception of God in the Future World is totally beyond our present grasp. That of the least of us will pale the achievements of the greatest sages in this world. Still, of course, it will be impossible to perceive God in His entirety. This is impossible for any being other than God Himself. Although incomparable to anything in this life, our perception will still be less than a drop in an infinite ocean. Nevertheless, it will far exceed anything possible in this world.[37]

In order that we may approach Him, God created a dimension of nearness to His being. By moving through this dimension, we are able to come closer and closer to God, even though we can never actually reach Him. This dimension is what we call the spiritual world. Our sages call the highest spiritual world *Atzilus* — the World of Nearness. All the spiritual worlds were created as vehicles through which we may draw near to God. In a sense, they serve as a filter, allowing us to draw near, and still not be obliterated by His infinite Light.[38]

In a number of places, our sages speak of these worlds as the Celestial Treasuries. Thus, Israel sings of God (*Song of Songs 1:4*), "The King will bring me into His chamber." Our sages comment that God will bring the righteous into His celestial chambers and allow them to probe the treasuries on high.[39]

This is also the meaning of the light that was made on the first day of creation. Our sages teach us that it was not mere physical light, but a wondrous light with which one could see "from one end of the universe to the other."[40] This was the light of perception, shining in all the spiritual worlds, with which one could experience this vision of God. Our sages thus continue, "God set this light aside for the righteous in the World to Come."[41]

This is the light of perception with which we will partake of the Divine — the "radiance of the Divine Presence." Elihu was speaking of this when he told Job (*Job 33:30*) that God will "turn back his soul from destruction, and light him with the light of life." The wise Solomon tells us that this light is the source of eternal life, when he says (*Proverbs 16:15*), "In the light of the King's face is life...."[43]

God's ultimate goal in creation was therefore the World to Come, where man could perceive a vision of God. Not God Himself, of course, but a vision. Perhaps through many filters, but still, a vision of God. The Psalmist sings of this vision (*Psalm 17:15*), "In righteousness, I will see Your face, when I awake, I will be satisfied with a vision of You." The Psalmist is speaking of the time when he will awake to the delights of the Future World. Our sages comment on this verse, "God will satisfy the righteous with a vision of the Divine Presence."[44]

The bliss of the Future World will be endless. In His endless goodness, God will give us a world of good without end. The Psalmist is speaking of this when he exclaims (*Psalm 16:11*), "In Your presence is fullness of joy, in Your right hand is bliss forever."[45]

Of course, everything about this Future World is totally beyond our powers of description. Even the visions of the greatest prophets will pale in comparison. It is something that no human mind can possibly imagine in this life. It cannot come through human understanding, but only as a gift from God, and when He gives it, we will understand. The prophet therefore says when speaking of the World to Come (*Isaiah 64:3*), "Never has the ear heard it—no eye has seen it—other than God: what He will do for those who hope in Him."[46]

III

THE CREATURE DESTINED by God to bring about this ultimate purpose is man. It is man who will enjoy this ultimate closeness to God in the Future World, and thereby fulfill God's purpose in creation. He therefore tells us through His prophet (*Isaiah 45:12*), "I have made the earth, and have created man upon it."

Every man must personally look upon himself as a partner with God in fulfilling this purpose. Creation exists for the sake of man, and it is man's duty to work toward fulfilling God's goal. Our sages thus teach us that every man should say, "The world was created for my sake."[47]

The Talmud provides us with an excellent example. A king once built a lavish palace, decorating it beautifully, and stocking it with the best food and drink. When it was all finished he invited his guests, saying, "If there are no guests, then what pleasure does the king have with all the good things that he has prepared?"[48]

It is for this reason that God made man last in the order of creation. All the world had to be prepared for its special guest. After everything had been prepared, the guest — man — was brought into the world.[49]

One may wonder how God can consider man. God is King over the entire universe, billions of light years in diameter, containing hundreds of billions of galaxies and quadrillions of suns. How can such a God care about man? How can he place His goal of creation on a mere speck of cosmic dust that we call our planet earth?

This question was actually first raised by the Psalmist. It might have been on a clear night, and as he gazed at the heavens, he saw them illuminated with a myriad of stars, and realized how small man really is. He then burst forth in song (*Psalm 8:4-6*):

> When I look at Your heavens,
> The work of Your fingers,
> The moon and stars
> That You have established —
> What is man that You think of him?
> Mortal man that You remember him?
> Yet, You have made him little less than God,
> You have crowned him with glory and splendor.

We know that God exists independent of space. It is therefore not too difficult to imagine that size alone is of little consequence to Him.

However, we also know that man is among the most complex things in all the universe. There is nothing that we know that is more complex than the human brain. It is infinitely more complex than even the largest galaxy. The brain of the smallest infant is vastly more wonderful than all the visible stars. It is little wonder that the Psalmist introduces his question with the remark (*ibid. 8:3*), "From the mouths of babes and sucklings, You have founded strength." He is providing the answer even before he asks the question. The heavens and stars may be awe inspiring, but a single word uttered by a child is vastly more wonderful.

Besides being complex, man is also the most aware thing in the universe. He is both perceptive and introspective. Even the stars and galaxies cannot match him in this. Since these are things that really matter to God, it is not so very surprising that He thinks of us.[50]

Beyond this, man is unique in creation because of his divine soul. In one place, Job says (*Job 31:2*), "What is a portion from God on high?" He is here speaking of the human soul, which is called "a portion from God on high." Man's soul comes from the highest possible of Godly levels, and is therefore a portion of the Divine.[51]

The Torah describes the creation of man with the words (*Genesis 2:7*), "God formed man of the dust of the earth, and He breathed into his nostrils a living soul." Our sages tell us that the Torah uses the expression "He breathed" for a very special reason. Just as human breath comes from the inner recesses of the body, so the human soul comes from the innermost depths of the Divine. Man's soul is therefore nothing less than a breath of God.[52]

The deeper meaning of this is that man's soul was God's very first thought and ultimate goal in creation. As such, it is closer to Him than anything else. In order to express this closeness, we call the soul a breath of God.

More than anything else, it is this soul that makes man unique in creation.[53] It is closer and more meaningful to God than any star or galaxy. In a spiritual sense, we may say that a single human soul is even greater than the entire physical universe. This is what the Talmud means when it says, "The deeds of the righteous are greater than the creation of heaven and earth."[54]

IV

IN ORDER TO make man a vehicle to accept His good, God created him with the capacity to enjoy. There are many things that give man pleasure. There are bodily pleasures, such as eating and drinking. There are mental pleasures, such as looking at beautiful art, reading a good book, or listening to fine music. But above all these is the pleasure of accomplishment. There are few human pleasures greater than those of accomplishment — of completing a job well done. Whether it is in doing good to others, solving a difficult problem, or simply doing the right thing, man experiences a certain glow of pleasure that is beyond comparison. The only thing that might come close is the spiritual pleasure of the mystic vision. Indeed, we find that many people are willing to forego the greatest physical pleasures in order to pursue a meaningful goal.[55]

For most of us, there is a glow of accomplishment that accompanies a meaningful act itself. If we are praised for it, the pleasure is all the greater. If an important person were to tell us that we had done something good, we would experience an even greater pleasure in accomplishment. To win, for example, a Nobel prize and be recognized by the world, is indeed one of the great pleasures of life, and there are people who would work a lifetime toward this end.

Accomplishment and recognition are among the natural pleasures of man. They are not physical pleasures, but delights of the spirit. The wise Solomon spoke of them when he said (*Proverbs 13:12*), "Desire fulfilled is a tree of life." He reiterates this several verses later, saying (*ibid. 13:19*), "Desire accomplished is sweet to the soul."

If the President were to summon you and tell you that you had done something good, you would feel great pride in accomplishment. How then would you feel if you were told this by some One much greater? What if God Himself were to tell you that you were doing something good and beneficial? How great would be your feeling of accomplishment?

In a sense, man's ultimate reward for doing good is this sense of accomplishment. God Himself tells us what is good, and the reward is in ultimately knowing that one has obeyed God's direct command. What greater accomplishment can there be than to act as a partner in the very purpose of creation?

It is for this reason that God revealed His will to man. He revealed the Torah to us, telling us what is good. When man then lives by the Torah and does what God Himself has defined as good, he can feel that he has accomplished one of the most meaningful things possible. God teaches us the way in order that we may achieve this everlasting bliss. This is what the Psalmist means when he says (*Psalm 16:11*), "You make me know the path of life; in Your presence is a fullness of joy, in Your right hand, everlasting bliss."[56]

The very fact that God revealed what is good to us provides us with the essence of its reward. Our sages thus teach us, "Greater is one who does something that he is commanded to do, than one who does what he is not commanded to do."[57] The very fact that it is commanded by God makes it all the more valued.

Our sages also explain this concept in a somewhat different light, teaching us that one who gives a gift to another must tell him about it. They derive this from the fact that God told us how great were the commandments that He was giving us. Rashi explains the reason for this, saying that when one is informed about a gift, then he both realizes its importance and is not ashamed to accept it.[58] Both of these concepts also apply here. The fact that God Himself tells us that certain things are good makes us realize their importance. Furthermore, as we shall presently see, it also prevents us from being ashamed of the good that God will give us.

The vehicle through which God defined what is good and beneficial is the Torah. When we obey the commandments of the Torah, we know that we are doing something that God commanded. In this way, we are then able to accept God's own goodness and fulfill His purpose in creation. The Torah is therefore the prime vehicle of God's purpose, and our sages thus teach us that the world was created for the sake of the Torah.[59]

The pleasure in accomplishment is not something that God gives us, but essentially something that we create ourselves. We ourselves therefore generate the good that God gives us. Our sages therefore teach us that virtue is its own reward.[60] The Prophet expresses this idea when he says (*Isaiah 3:10*), "Say to the righteous that it shall be good, for he shall eat the fruit of his deeds."[61] In another place our sages put it this way: "Today to act, tomorrow to receive reward."[62]

This concept is expressed most clearly by the words of Rabbi Chiya in the Talmud. He says, "Enjoying the fruits of your labor is better than the fear of heaven. It is thus written (*Psalm 128:2*), 'You shall eat the fruit of your effort—you shall be happy, and it shall be well with you.' 'You shall be happy'—in this world—'and it shall be well with you'—in the World to Come."[63]

What Rabbi Chiya is saying is that the main good of the Future World is the enjoyment of the fruits of one's labor. This is what he means when he says that "it shall be well with you in the World to Come." This, he says, is greater than mere "fear of heaven." As we discussed earlier, "fear of heaven" refers to our knowledge and perception of God. This perception may be a great thing, but it is all the greater when it comes as the fruit of our own efforts.

The opposite of pleasure is pain. Here again, we have both physical pain and mental anguish. Among the worst possible kinds of psychological pain are the feelings of guilt and shame. In one place, our sages say that the pain of shame is as great as that of death.[64]

A number of our great teachers write that the fire of *Gehenom*, the ultimate punishment for evil, is actually the burning shame that one experiences when he stands naked before God with all his sins revealed.[65]

Imagine standing before God, with your memory wide open and with no way to escape. We all know the terrible shame and humiliation of being caught doing wrong. Imagine what it is like when the One who catches you is God Himself. This is shame without comparison.

It is of this shame that Daniel is speaking when he says (*Daniel 12:2*),

"Many who sleep in the dust shall awake, some to everlasting life, and some to everlasting shame." The Prophet also speaks of this, saying (*Isaiah 66:24*), "They shall go forth and look upon the carcasses of the men who have rebelled against Me. For their worms shall not die, neither shall their fire be quenched — they shall be ashamed before all flesh."[66]

But there is another kind of shame that is even more basic. This is the shame of having to accept a free gift. This is a very primeval shame, deeply seated in man's psyche. Our sages thus teach us, "One who eats another's bread is ashamed to look in his face."[67] From the context of this saying, we see that it not only applies to human psychology, but even to the most primitive things in nature.

Our sages repeat this lesson any number of times. They teach us that "when a man must depend on gifts, his face changes."[68] In another place, they say, "When one depends on the gifts of others, the world appears dark to him."[69] Elsewhere they proclaim, "One who eats at another's table is never satisfied."[70]

God wanted the good that He would give to be perfect good, not tinged by any shame. If it were given as a free gift, however, it would always be accompanied by the shame that results from accepting a free gift. The only way to avoid this would be for the good to be earned, so that it would no longer be a gift. It is for this reason that the good that God gives us is only bestowed as a reward for our own actions.

When the Zohar speaks of the ultimate world of good, it says, "Happy is he who comes here without shame."[71] This is actually echoing the words of the Prophet, who said (*Jeremiah 2:26*), "And you shall eat and be satisfied...and my people shall never be ashamed."

V

IN ORDER THAT man enjoy the pleasure of his accomplishment, it is imperative that he know that he acted as a matter of free choice, rather than through compulsion. It is for this reason that God gave us free will. We bear full responsibility for our action and full credit for the good we do. We are free to choose between good and evil. This is what makes the choice of good a true accomplishment.[72]

If man did not have free will, then he would be little more than a puppet or a robot. Both a robot and a puppet can accomplish things, but they cannot have any feeling of accomplishment. They are mere machines. In a sense, it is free will that makes us more than a machine. If man did not have free will, his accomplishment would be no more than that of a robot. There would be no feeling of pride or pleasure in it at all.

We can therefore say that free will is required by God's justice.[73] In a deeper sense, we must say that it is required by God's very purpose in creation. For the good that God desired to grant to His world is essentially bestowed as a result of our free will. We can therefore say that free will is one of the most essential ingredients of all creation.[74]

But there is a much deeper way of looking at the concept of free will, and it follows as a direct result of our previous discussion. As discussed earlier, the greatest good that God could give is Himself. The purpose of creation was therefore to give man a chance to come close to God.

When we speak of coming close to God, we are not speaking of physical closeness. God exists in a realm far beyond the mere physical. When we speak of closeness to God, we are speaking of spiritual closeness.

We said earlier that this spiritual closeness involves knowledge and perception of God. But on a deeper level, this is really a result of our closeness to Him. For we cannot know God by looking at Him. We cannot even know Him by meditating or contemplating about Him. There are no symbols in our minds which we can use to even think of God. Philosophy is equally futile, and for the same reason. We can only extend our thoughts beyond the immediate, using symbols and concepts that we can conceive. But God is utterly beyond our conception. Therefore, the only way in which we can know God and perceive Him is by coming close to Him in a spiritual sense.

But what is closeness in a nonphysical sense?

We find a hint in the words of our sages. The Torah states (*Deuteronomy 13:5*), "You shall follow the Lord your God, fear Him and keep His commandments, obey Him and serve Him, and bind yourself to Him." The Talmud asks, "How can one bind himself to God? Is it not written (*Deuteronomy 9:3*), 'The Lord your God is a consuming fire?'" The Talmud answers that we bind ourselves to God by imitating His attributes.[75]

What the Talmud is teaching us is that in a spiritual sense, closeness is resemblance. Two things that resemble each other are close in a spiritual sense. Things that differ are distant. The more two things resemble each other, the closer they are spiritually.

This is expressed even more clearly in the Midrash,[77] commenting on the verse (*Leviticus 19:2*), "You shall be holy, for I, the Lord your God am holy." The Midrash tells us that this passage explains two other passages: (*Deuteronomy 4:4*), "You, who have bound yourselves to God, arc all living today," and (*Jeremiah 13:11*), "As a loincloth clings to a man's waist, so shall the whole house of Judah cling to Me."

Although the Midrash does not openly state it, it is asking the same question as the Talmud did above. What does the Torah mean when it says that "you have bound yourselves to God," or that the people shall "cling" to Him? The Midrash therefore tells us that these passages are explained by the verse, "You shall be holy, for I am Holy." We bind ourselves to God by working to resemble Him in His holiness. For in a spiritual sense, the more two things resemble each other, the closer they are.

We can now understand the reason for free will in a deeper sense.

As we discussed earlier, the good that God's plan has destined for His world is the ultimate good, namely God Himself. His plan is to give a creature, namely man, the opportunity to draw close to Him.

But when we speak of giving such good, we immediately face a dilemma. God is the giver and man is the receiver, and as such, they are two opposites. In a spiritual sense, they are as far from each other as north and south. Giver and receiver are exact opposites. As long as man is a mere receiver, he stands at the opposite pole away from God, the Giver. In a spiritual sense, man and God would then be ultimately distant from each other.

Therefore, God arranged things so that man himself would be the creator of good.

God made man in such a way that he too can create good. Man does so every time he obeys God's commandments. In doing so, he draws God's light to his own being, and thus, rather than being a mere receiver, he becomes a partner with God. The good that man ultimately receives is therefore as much the result of his own efforts as it is a gift of God.

Man therefore receives God's good by himself doing good, thereby resembling God in the greatest degree possible. For man draws close to God by imitating Him, and when he does so, he can be a recipient of God's good. This is what the Psalmist meant when he sang (*Psalm 125:4*), "God is good to the good." In order to receive God's goodness, one must himself be good. Our sages interpret this verse by saying, "Let he who is good, come and accept good, from He who is good to the good."[78]

In order for this resemblence to be in any way complete, man had to be created with free will. Just as God acts as a free Being, so does man. Just as He operates without prior restraint, so does man. Just as God does good as a matter of His own choice, so does man. According to many commentators, this is one meaning of man having been created in the "image of God."[79]

We can experience a glimmer of this closeness to God, even in the physical world. The pleasure of accomplishment that we experience when doing good is a touch of this closeness. It is a pure spiritual pleasure, and as such is a reflection of the ultimate spiritual pleasure, namely, closeness to God. When we accomplish good, we are imitating God and bringing Him close to us, and therefore feel an inkling of this pleasure.[80]

On the other hand, the ultimate spiritual pain is being separated from God. This explains the psychological pain experienced when one is forced to accept charity from others. When one is a taker rather than a giver, then he is ultimately far from God, the Giver.

Our sages therefore describe this feeling as shame. They say that if God were to give us His good as a free gift, then we would experience shame in accepting it. For what is shame? Most often, it involves being caught in an improper situation. A person experiences shame when he is caught doing something that he should not or when he finds himself in an improper place. But for a mere receiver to be close to God is also an improper place. Therefore, we describe this feeling as one of shame.

VI

As we have said, one of the ultimate goals of man is the imitation of God. We do this in every good act, paralleling God's own creation of good. The most direct way that we can do this, however, is in our actions toward our fellow man.

God's purpose in creation could have been fulfilled with the creation of a single creature to accept His good. Such a creature, however, could never truly resemble God. God Himself is a bestower of good, and if only one creature existed, then to whom would it do good? Certainly not to God, for God has no needs. It is for this reason that God created the world as an arena for an entire species of man.

When God first created man, Adam was one. God then said (*Genesis 2:18*), "It is not good for man to be alone; I will make him a helper as his counterpart." As long as man was alone, he could not really be good. For to be good is to imitate God, the giver of good. A man alone would have no one to whom to bestow good, and therefore, could not be called "good." This is what God meant when He said, "It is not *good* for man to be alone."

God then created woman as a counterpart of man. The relationship between man and woman would be very much the same as that of God to the world. It is for this reason that we always refer to God in the masculine gender, since He is the active creative force in the world.[81] God is the archetype of the masculine and His creation is that of the feminine. Woman was therefore created from man, just as the world came from God.

Man can become a partner of God in the procreation of children.

Just as God is a creator, so man also becomes a creator of life. Our sages therefore teach us that there are three partners in the procreation of a child, his father, his mother and God.[82] The sexual act is the vehicle through which man displays this aspect of his partnership with God, and this is one reason why its perversion is considered among the worst of sins.[83]

In a spiritual sense, the good that man does also benefits every other human being. Thus, in doing good, one is at least indirectly benefiting his fellow man, even in the case of ritual laws that do not directly do so. Our sages thus teach us that every single Jew is morally responsible for every other.[84] The author of *Reshis Chochmah*[85] explains that all souls are bound together, as with a rope, and the movement of one is reflected in every other. This is what the Torah means when it says (*Numbers 16:22*), "One man sins, and anger is directed against the entire community."

The Midrash provides us with an excellent example illustrating this:[86] A number of people are sitting in a small boat. All of a sudden, one man begins to drill a hole under his seat. When the people complain, he retorts, "What complaint do you have? After all, I'm drilling the hole under my own seat." Finally, a wise man answers him, "We are all in the same boat. The hole may be under your seat, but the water that comes in will make the boat sink with all of us."

In a spiritual sense, we are all in the same boat. Every good thing that we do affects all mankind, and the same is true of all evil. In every good act that we do, we imitate God insofar that we ultimately bring good to all humanity. This is indeed one reason why God put us all in the same spiritual boat.

Of course, we do this more directly when we do good toward our fellow man. This is the archetype of all good. There is no way of imitating God more closely than in doing good to others.

In the previous section, we quoted the Talmud as saying that we bind ourselves to God by imitating His ways. But in what ways does the Talmud say that we imitate God? Look at its words carefully:[87]

> Just as God clothes the naked, so shall you.
> Just as God visits the sick, so shall you.
> Just as God comforts the bereaved, so shall you.

In another place, the Talmud says that we must also imitate God in His mercy and compassion.[88] The general lesson is that we resemble God most in our relationship with our fellow human beings.

This concept is best exemplified by the famous story of Hillel.[89] The Talmud tells us that a non-Jew once came to Hillel and said, "I wish to convert to Judaism, but only if you teach me the entire Torah while I stand on one foot."

Hillel replied, "What is hateful to you, do not do to your fellow man. This is the core of Judaism. The rest is mere commentary."

Many of the commentators find this story very perplexing. The commandments dealing with our relationship toward our fellow man are certainly very important. But there are also many other important commandments that apparently have nothing at all to do with other people. How could Hillel have dismissed these as mere commentary?

What Hillel was teaching us, however, was that the main reason for all the commandments is the imitation of God, and that this is exemplified by our relations with our fellow human beings. We must deal with our fellows just as God deals with us. In doing so, we fulfill His purpose in creation. This imitation of God is ultimately the purpose of all the commandments.

This is also the meaning of what God told His prophet (*Jeremiah 22:16*), "He judged the cause of the poor and the needy, and it was well. Is this not to know Me?" As discussed earlier, we can only know God by drawing close to Him through imitating Him. God is telling us that the main way in which we know Him is by imitating Him in doing good to others.

There is a commandment in the Torah (*Leviticus 19:18*), "You shall love your neighbor like yourself." One of our foremost leaders, Rabbi Akiba, said, "This commandment is the core of the Torah."[90] Rabbi Akiba is teaching us the same lesson as Hillel. We imitate God's love for the world through our love toward our fellow man. In this way, we draw ourselves close to God and fulfill His purpose in creation.

In a deeper sense, the concept of love itself is the archetype of spiritual closeness. Where a bond of love exists between two people, they are close—even though they may be separated by vast distances.[91] On the other hand, people who hate each other are far apart, even when they are sitting right next to each other. Love and hate exist in a spiritual, rather than a physical dimension. Love between two people implies a harmony and complementarity between them. It is this harmony that makes them close, irrespective of physical distance. In obeying God's commandments, we seek to bring a similar harmony and closeness between ourselves and God. "You shall love your neighbor as yourself" is therefore indeed the prime rule of the Torah. It not only leads us to a closeness to God, but also teaches us the meaning of such closeness.[92]

Following a similar line of reasoning, we can understand what our sages mean when they teach us, "He who denies the doing of kindness (*Gemilus Chasadim*) is like one who denies the most fundamental principle (God Himself)." God is the ultimate bestower of kindness, and one who divorces himself from such deeds, places himself poles apart from God. God is the ultimate doer of good, and this man denies doing good. He is therefore said to be like one who divorces himself from God.

God is the source of all life, and therefore, the more one resembles God, the more he partakes of life. One who clings to God is said to be truly alive, as the Torah says (*Deuteronomy 4:4*), "You who have clung to God, are all alive today." One who divorces himself from God, on the other hand, is considered dead.

This is the meaning of what the wise Solomon said (*Proverbs 15:27*), "He who hates gifts shall live." For God is a giver, never a receiver. When one refuses to become a receiver, he resembles God in this respect, and is thus considered alive. The more one gives, the more he resembles God in this respect. We thus find (*Proverbs 10:2*), "Charity saves from death." When one gives, he resembles his Creator, the source of all life.

One who does not resemble God, on the other hand, is counted among the dead. Thus, for example, our sages teach us that the poor man who lives off charity is counted among the dead.[93] In this sense, such a man is poles apart from God, since God is a Giver, and this poor man only takes. The same is true of one who does not have any children.

In a similar vein, our sages teach us, "The wicked are called dead, even during their lifetime."[94] In being wicked, they are ultimately separated from God, the source of all life. They are therefore considered dead, even while they are still walking and breathing. They may be alive in a physical sense, but in a spiritual sense, they are no longer among the living.

VII

ONE OF THE fundamental principles of creation is therefore free will, where man can choose good as a matter of his own choice. God's purpose in creation does not allow man to be a robot or a puppet.

But if God's purpose does not allow man to be a robot, neither does it permit him to be a prisoner.

Just as man must have free will, so must he have the opportunity to make use of it. A man locked up in prison may have the same free will as anyone else, but there is little that he can do with it. If man is to do good as a matter of free choice, he must also have the possibility of doing that which is not good. For man to resemble his Creator to the greatest possible extent, he must exist in an arena where he has the maximum freedom of choice. The more that man resembles God in His omnipotence, the closer he can resemble Him in his free choice to do good.

It is for this reason that God created the possibility of evil.[95]

God therefore told His prophet (*Isaiah 45:7*), "I form light and create darkness, I make peace and create evil. I am God, I do all these things." In keeping himself from evil, man takes the first step toward good.[96] Job thus said (*Job 28:28*), "The fear of God is wisdom, and to depart from evil is understanding."[97] God created evil in order that it may be conquered.

If nothing but good were possible, it would produce no benefit. To use the Talmudic metaphor, it would be like carrying a lamp in broad daylight.[98] The *Zohar* states, "The advantage of wisdom comes from foolishness, just as that of light would not be discernible, and would

66

produce no benefit. Thus, it is written (*Ecclesiastes 7:14*), 'God has made one thing opposite the other.'"99

Ultimately, there is one Source of everything that exists, even evil. It is not that God actually created evil, but it is through His will that the possibility of evil exists.100 Everything comes from God and must return to Him.101 In the meanwhile, however, evil exists in order to be conquered.

The *Zohar* gives us a very excellent example explaining this.102 A king once wanted to give his son greater responsibility. Before doing this, however, he wanted to test his loyalty. What did the king do? He hired a temptress to try to persuade the son to rebel against his father. She was to use all her wiles to tempt the boy to go against his father.

Whether or not this temptress succeeds, she is still a servant of the king, doing his will. Even if she succeeds in persuading the son to go against his father, she is still doing what the king bid her. The same is true of evil. Ultimately it exists to fulfill God's purpose.

As discussed earlier, the closeness to God resulting from our good deeds is reflected in our satisfaction of accomplishment accompanying such acts. However, such satisfaction is enhanced according to the difficulty of the accomplishment. Our sages thus teach us, "The greater the suffering, the greater the reward."103

The Midrash illustrates this with another example.104 A king once wanted to know which of his subjects really loved and respected him. He built an iron wall around his palace. He then proclaimed, "Let those who really love and respect the king come to the palace." Those who were truly loyal scaled the iron wall and thus showed their loyalty.

This wall of iron represents the forces of evil in the world. God makes it all the more difficult for us to approach Him in order to increase our ultimate reward. This is expressed quite well in another Midrash:105

Another king wanted to test the loyalty of his subjects. He built a high wall around his palace, and then placed a very narrow opening in it. All those who wanted to see the king had to squeeze themselves through this very narrow opening.

Of course, there is one major difference between God and the earthly king in the example. God knows and does not have to find out. The reason why He creates these barriers, however, is to bring out our own good potential into action.[106] In this way, He enhances our feeling of satisfaction of accomplishment, and ultimately, our reward.

This world was therefore created as a place of maximum challenge. For the greater the challenge, the greater the reward. This of course may result in many who do not overcome the challenge. Still, even they will receive reward for the good that they do. Ultimately, however, the world was created for the sake of those who overcome their challenge. Our sages thus teach us that the universe was created for the sake of the righteous.[107] As the *Sefer HaYashar* puts it, the good are like the fruit, while the evil men are like the husks. Both may grow on the same tree, but only the fruit fulfills its purpose.[108]

This is the meaning of a question disputed in the Talmud:[109] For two and a half years, there was a dispute between Shammai's school and that of Hillel. Shammai's school contended that it would have been better for man never to have been created. The school of Hillel said that it was better for man to have been created. After two and a half years, they finally agreed and decided that man would have been better off if he had not been created. But now that he is created, let him be very careful what he does in this world.

It is indeed a gamble for man to have to descend to this world of temptation. One might argue that it would have been better for God to grant man a less complete good and not make him earn it. This is the dispute between the schools of Shammai and Hillel. The good that man receives is greatly enhanced by virtue of his having earned it. Still, coming to this world is a great gamble. It is a place of the greatest of temptations. If a man was given an initial choice, perhaps it would be best for him to choose a lesser good, without taking the gamble of coming to this world of evil. This was the contention of Shammai's school. The school of Hillel, on the other hand, maintained that the good realized makes the gamble worthwhile.

Ultimately, we are taught that one cannot depend on a wager.[110] They therefore finally decided that it would have been better for man not to have taken the gamble of having been born into this world. This contention is supported by the words of the wise Solomon (*Ecclesiastes 4:2–3*), "I count the dead happy because they are dead, happier than the living who are still in life. Happier than both is the man yet unborn, who has not seen the evil that is done under the sun."[111]

When a man dies, he no longer faces the challenge of evil in this world. Better yet, however, is he who is not yet born. It would be better for him never to have to take the gamble, struggling against the evil of this world. Solomon therefore concludes (*ibid. 4:6*), "Better a handful of repose, than two hands full of effort and chasing the wind."

VIII

THERE ARE TWO basic concepts in human existence. First, man must earn the good that God has prepared. Secondly, he must receive this good.

There is, however, a basic difference between the environment needed for these two concepts. While earning the reward, we must have the maximum possible challenge. This in turn gives us the greatest possible satisfaction in accomplishment. Such an environment must therefore be one where neither God Himself, nor the divine nature of our good deeds, is obvious. It must be a world where God is hidden, and where good is only accomplished with the greatest difficulty.

The place where man recieves good, on the other hand, must be the exact opposite. In order for man to enjoy the maximum possible satisfaction from the good that he has done, the true nature of his deeds must be as obvious as possible. The existence of God must also be as apparent as possible in such a world. It must be a place where man realizes the goodness of his deeds and their relationship to God.

It is for this reason that God created two levels of existence.[112] First there is this world—*Olam HaZeh*—a place of accomplishment and maximum challenge. Secondly, there is the World to Come—*Olam HaBah*—the world of ultimate reward, where both God's existence and the nature of one's deeds are totally apparent.

IX

BOTH THIS WORLD and the World to Come exist on a physical plane. This is obvious in the case of the physical world. However, according to most authorities, the Future World will also be physical. This is the reason for our belief in the resurrection of the dead. It is a foundation of our faith that God will ultimately bring the dead back to life, or at least provide the souls of the dead with bodies like their previous ones.[113] It will be in these resurrected bodies that man will partake of his ultimate reward in the World to Come.[114]

But why is a physical world necessary at all? Since both God and His ultimate good are spiritual, what need is there for a physical body?

Before we can answer this question, we must first ask another question. What is the difference between the material and the spiritual?

We speak of the material and the spiritual as two different concepts. We know that the spiritual is not material. But precisely what is the difference?

The answer should be obvious. The main difference between the material and spiritual involves space. Physical space only exists in the physical world. In the spiritual, there is no space as we know it.

As discussed earlier, the concept of distance and closeness also exist in the spiritual world. They do not refer to physical distance, since this does not exist in the spiritual realm. As we have mentioned earlier, however, closeness in a spiritual sense involves resemblance. Two things that resemble each other are said to be spiritually close. Two things that differ, on the other hand, are far apart in a spiritual sense.

This has very important implications. In the spiritual world, it is utterly impossible to bring two opposites together. Because they are opposite, they are by definition, poles apart.

Thus, for example, God and man are worlds apart—"as the heavens are higher than the earth." On a purely spiritual plane, it would be totally impossible for the two ever to be brought together.

It was for this reason that God created the concept of space. Spiritual things can be bound to the material, just as for example the soul is bound to the body.

Two opposites can then be brought together by being bound to physical objects. In the physical world, space exists, and two opposites can literally be pushed together. Furthermore, two spiritual opposites can even be bound to the same material object.[115]

Thus, for example, man has both an urge for good and an urge for evil, the *Yetzer Tov*, and the *Yetzer HaRa*. In a purely spiritual sense, these are poles apart. Without a physical world, they could never be brought together in a single entity.

The archetype of the spiritual being is the angel. Since an angel has no body, it can never contain both good and evil in its being. Our sages therefore teach us that angels have no *Yetzer HaRa*.[116]

It is only in a physical being that both good and evil can exist together. Although they are at opposite poles spiritually, they can come together in the physical man. One reason why God created man in a physical world was therefore to allow him to have full freedom of choice, with both good and evil as part of his makeup. Without a physical world, these two concepts could never exist in the same being.[117]

The fact that good and evil can exist in the same physical space also allows good to overcome evil in this world. Here again, this is only possible in a physical world. In a purely spiritual arena, good could never come close enough to evil to have any influence over it. In the physical world, however, good and evil can exist together, and good can therefore overcome evil. Our sages thus teach us that one of the main reasons why man was placed in the physical world was to overcome the forces of evil.[118] The *Zohar* expresses it by stating that we are here "to turn darkness into light."[119]

The entire concept of the nonphysical is very difficult to comprehend, and may be clarified by a remarkable teaching of our sages. The

Midrash tells us, "One angel cannot have two missions. Neither can two angels share the same mission."[120]

This teaching brings our entire discussion into focus. The angel is the archetype of the nonphysical being. When we speak of an angel, we are speaking of an entity that exists purely on a spiritual plane. Angels can be differentiated only by their mission, that is, by their involvement and attachment to some physical thing.

Two angels therefore cannot share the same mission. It is only their different missions that make the two angels different entities. They cannot be separated by space like physical objects.[121] Therefore, if they both had the same mission, there would be nothing to differentiate them, and they would be one.

Similarly, one angel cannot have two missions. On a purely spiritual plane, two different concepts cannot exist in a single entity. If an angel had two missions, then it would be two angels.

We can also understand this in terms of the human mind. In a sense, the mind is a pure spiritual entity, bound to man's physical brain. Many thoughts and memories may be bound together by man's physical brain, but the mind can only focus on one of them at a time. In simple terms, a person can only think of one thing at a time. A thought is a spiritual entity, and as such, can only contain a single concept. Since both a thought and an angel are basic spiritual entities, this is very closely related to the fact that an angel can only have a single mission.[122]

For a similar reason, angels have no way of knowing anything that does not pertain to their particular mission. An angel may be created initially with a vast storehouse of knowledge, but it has no way of increasing it, at least, not beyond its own sphere of activity. Thus, for example, we find one angel asking another a question (*Daniel 12:6*): "And one [angel] said to the Man dressed in linen...'How long shall it be until the end of these wonders?'" One angel had to ask the other, because he himself could not know something outside of his own domain.[123]

In the physical world, we can learn things through our five senses. We can see, hear, feel, smell and taste. Our knowledge of things comes from our physical proximity to them. In the spiritual world, however, this does not exist. The only way that one can learn about a thing is to come into spiritual proximity with it. An angel cannot do this outside of his own realm.

Man therefore has an advantage over an angel. The very fact that he exists in this lower world enables him to reach up ever higher.

There are concepts of good decreed by God, and as His decrees, they are intimately bound to Him. When a man physically involves himself with these good concepts, he literally binds himself to God. He thus achieves a closeness that no angel could ever hope to reach.[124]

This is a major difference between a man and an angel. An angel is assigned to one spiritual station, and has no way to rise any higher. Thus, when the Prophet speaks of angels, he says (*Isaiah 6:2*), "Around Him, the seraphim stood." Angels are described as standing and stationary. But when God speaks to man, He tells him (*Zechariah 3:7*), "If you walk in My ways... then I will give you a place to move among those who stand here." God was showing the Prophet a vision of stationary angels, and telling him that he would be able to move among them. Man can move from level to level, but angels are bound to their particular plane.[125]

There are many different levels in the spiritual world. The Talmud thus speaks of angels called *Chayos*, and says:[126]

> The distance between heaven and earth
>   is five hundred years.
> The width of each heaven
>   is five hundred years.
> This is true of each of the seven heavens.
> The feet of the Chayos are as great as them all.
> The ankles of the Chayos are as great
>   as everything below them.
> The shins of the Chayos are equally great.
> The thighs of the Chayos are equally great.
> The hips of the Chayos are equally great.
> The body of the Chayos is equally great.
> The neck of the Chayos is equally great.
> The head of the Chayos is equally great.
> The horns of the Chayos are equally great.

> The legs of the Throne of Glory (*Kisey HaKavod*)
> are as great as everything below them.
> The throne itself is equally great.

Here we see the many levels of the spiritual world, and the Kabbalists speak of many other levels. In a purely spiritual sense, there is no way for these to come together. The only thing that in any way unifies them is their relationship to the physical world.

In order to reach the highest levels of holiness, man must therefore become part of the physical world. When he obeys God's commandments, he attaches himself to the same physical objects as the One who commanded them. In obeying the commandments, man therefore attaches himself to God to the greatest possible degree. He is thus able to scale the highest spiritual levels.

This is the symbolism of the ladder in Jacob's dream. The Torah tells us that Jacob saw (*Genesis 28:12*), "A ladder standing on earth, whose top reached the heavens." It is only through earthly deeds that we climb to the loftiest heights. The different levels of the spiritual world—the rungs of the "ladder"—can only be bound together when they are "standing on the earth."[127]

The *Zohar* therefore gives an interesting example explaining why the soul must descend to the physical world:[128] "A king once had a son. He sent him to a faraway village to grow and thereby learn the way of the king's palace. The same is true of the soul. It is sent far away to this world to learn the way of the King's palace."

In the light of our discussion this example becomes very clear. For it is only in this physical world that we can achieve any true closeness and perception of God.

In obeying the commandments, man brings God's light down to this world. The Midrash thus tells us that the reason that God created the physical world is because "He wanted to have a dwelling place below."[129] It is through the physical that God's light becomes connected with lower levels of creation.

Just as there are different levels in the spiritual world, so are there different levels in the human soul.[130] These levels extend to the highest spiritual domains. It is only through the body, however, that these different levels are united. Without the body, each would remain separated in its own level.

The main concept here is that spiritual unity is mainly a result of the physical. The *Zohar* expresses this concept, saying, "One who wishes to understand the concept of the holy unity should look at the flame rising from a coal or from a burning lamp. The flame is only unified when it is attached to a physical object."[131]

A flame also contains numerous levels. As in the case of the human soul, these parts can only be united when they are attached to a physical entity.

When a person dies, the different levels of the soul therefore separate. Death not only involves the separation of body and soul, but also the separation of the various parts of the soul. When they are not bound together by the body, each level acts as a separate entity.[132]

This is one reason why the World to Come will bring body and soul back together. A soul alone has no connection to its higher parts, and moreover, has no way of elevating itself. As such, it is no better than an angel. Between death and the resurrection, it remains in the "World of Souls" in what is primarily a static state.[133] It is only when it is reunited with the body that it can once again elevate itself. Of course, there is no challenge in the Future World, and therefore, this elevation is more tenuous than in this physical world. It therefore depends to a very large extent on the individual's previous preparation.

The Talmud therefore teaches us that the righteous have no rest, neither in this world nor in the next. They are constantly rising from one level to the next, as it is written (*Psalm 84:8*), "They go from strength to strength, every one appearing before God...."[134]

X

ALTHOUGH ALL THIS may seem very deep and complex, it is all really something very simple. It is merely a simple expression of God's love for us. It is for this reason that He gave us the Torah and its commandments. These too are an expression of His love. Our sages thus teach us that "God wanted to do good to Israel, and therefore gave them Torah and Commandments in abundance."[135]

When we realize this, we also know that our ultimate goal in life is to fulfill God's purpose. We must study God's Torah, and then follow its teachings. Only then can we find meaning in life.

This entire concept is expressed most beautifully in the prayer *Ahavas Olom*, part of the evening service:

> With an infinite world of love,
> You loved Your people Israel;
> You taught us Your Torah, Your Mitzvos,
> Your code, Your way.
> Therefore, O Lord our God,
> When we lie down and wake up
> We will think of Your teachings —
> Find happiness in Your Torah's words.
> For they are our life and length of days;
> We will follow them day and night,
> And Your love will never be taken from us.

Notes

1. *Cf. Sanhedrin* 39b, Rashi *ad loc. "Oder."*
2. *Zohar* 1:10b, 1:230b, 2:166b, *Sefer HaBris* 2:1:3. Also see *Emunos VeDeyos,* 1:4 end, 3:0, *Or HaShem* (Crescas) 2:6:2, *Sefer HaYashar* #1, *Pardes Rimonim* 2:6, *Etz Chaim, Shaar HaKelallim* #1, *Reshis Chochmah, Shaar HaTshuvah* #1, *Shnei Luchos HaBris, Bais Yisroel* (Jerusalem, 5720) 1:21b, *Shomrei Emunim (HaKadmon)* 2:13, *Derech HaShem* 1:2.1, *Likutey Moharan* #64.
3. Also see Psalms 106:1, 107:1, 118:1, 1 Chronicles 16:34, 2 Chronicles 20:21. From this, we see that it was a much repeated praise.
4. *Likutey Moharan* 52, *Akedas Yitzchok* 4 (35b). Also see *Yad, Yesodey HaTorah* 1:3. *Cf. Bemidbar Rabbah* 10:1.
5. See *Sefer Baal Shem Tov, Berashis* 6; *Magid Devarav LeYaakov* #102. *Cf. Bereshis Rabbah* 1:5, *Sh'mos Rabbah* 38:5.
6. *Bereshis Rabbah* 2:7.
7. *Moreh Nevuchim* 3:25.
8. *Berachos* 60a.
9. Rabbi Moshe Chaim Luzzatto, *KaLaCh Pischey Chochmah* #2.
10. *Yoma* 38a.
11. See *Avos* 6:11.
12. See *Moreh Nevuchim* 1:64, from Exodus 33:18.
13. *Moreh Nevuchim* 3:13; *Shamayim Chadishim* (Abarbanel) 4:6, quoted in *Shevil Emunah* (on *Emunos VeDeyos*) end of 1, #9; *Shomer Emunim* 2:13.
14. *Bereshis Rabbah* 1:2.
15. *Avos* 6:3, *Berachos* 5a, *Kallah* 8, *Yerushalmi Rosh HaShanah* 3:8, *Tanchuma Re'eh* 11, *Tana DeBei Eliahu Zuta* 17, *Pesicha Eicha Rabbah* 2.
16. *Pirkey DeRabbi Eliezer* 3.
17. *Likutey Moharan* 52. See *Zohar* 3:257b, *Etz Chaim, Drush Egolim VeYashar* #1; *Shevil Emunah*, beginning of #3.
18. *Sefer HaYashar* 1.
19. *Esther Rabbah* 10:14.

20. *Midrash Tehillim* 31. See *Derech HaShem* 1:2:1.
21. *Ibid.* 2:6:4; *Shiur Kumah* 13:3.
24. *Yerushalmi Berachos* 6:1 (41b). *Cf. Targum ad loc.*
25. *Moreh Nevuchim* 1:18.
26. *Zohar* 2:42b, *Emunos VeDeyos,* end of chapter 1, *Etz Chaim, Shaar HaKelallim* #1.
27. *Shiur Kumah* 13:3.
28. *Reshis Chochmah,* introduction. *Cf.* Rabenu Yonah on Proverbs 2:5.
29. *Shabbos* 31b.
30. *Berachos* 6b.
31. *Yad, Tshuvah* 8:7. *Cf. Berachos* 4a.
32. *Avos* 4:16.
33. *Kiddushin* 39b, *Chulin* 142a.
34. *Avos* 4:17.
35. *Berachos* 17a.
36. *Yad, Tshuvah* 8:3, *Toras HaAdam, Shaar HaGumul* (Jerusalem, 5723) p. 307.
37. *Daas Tevunah* (Tel Aviv, 5726) p. 9.
38. *Pardes Rimonim* 2:6, *Shefa Tal,* end of #2, *Etz Chaim, Shaar Derushey ABYA* #1.
39. Midrash, quoted in *Shaar HaGamul,* p. 296. See also *Zohar* 2:166a, *Likutey Moharan* 275, *Sichos HaRan* 134.
40. *Bereshis Rabbah* 12:5, *Chagigah* 12a.
41. *Ibid., Bereshis Rabbah* 3:6, Rashi on Genesis 1:4.
42. *Bahir* 160, *Shaar HaGamul* p. 306; *Avodas HaKodesh* 2:25.
43. *VaYikra Rabbah* 20:7, *Zohar* 1:135a.
44. *Baba Basra* 10a.
45. *Emunos VeDeyos* 9:5, Ibn Ezra *ad loc., VaYikra Rabbah* 30:2.
46. *Berachos* 34b, *Sanhedrin* 99a, Rashi, *Metzudos ad loc., Yad, Tshuvah* 8:7.
47. *Sanhedrin* 4:5 (37a).
48. *Ibid.* 38a, *Bereshis Rabbah* 8:5, *Emunos VeDeyos,* introduction to #4.
49. See *Bereshis Rabbah* 8:1, 19:4, *Tikuney Zohar* 6a, *Levush Techeles* #1, *Ikkarim* 1:11.
50. See *Emunos VeDeyos* 4:2, *Akedas Yitzchok* 5 (43a).
51. *Shefa Tal,* beginning of introduction; *Nishmas Chaim* 2:9, *Nefesh HaChaim* 1:15, *Likutey Amaram (Tanya)* 1:2 (6a); *Shaarey Kedushah* 3:2, *Likutey Torah HaAri* on Esodus 33:5; *Pischey Chochmah VoDaas, Biur Olom HaNikudos* (with *KaLach Pischey Chochmah,* Jerusalem, 5721) p. 23a.
52. *Zohar* 1:27a, 3:123b, *Zohar Chadash* 10c, *Likutey Amaram loc. cit., Ramban* on Genesis 2:7; *idem, D'rashah Toras HaShem Temimah* (in *Kisvey HaRamban,* Jerusalem, 5723) p. 159, *Shefa Tal* (Brooklyn, 5720) p. 4c in *Hagah, Shiu Kumah* 51.
53. For the question whether or not there is intelligent life on other worlds, see my article, "On Extraterrestrial Life" in *INTERCOM* 14:1, December, 1972.

54. *Kesubos* 5a.
55. See Rambam on *Sanhedrin* 10:1, *Ikkarim* 4:33.
56. Ibn Ezra *ad loc., Emunos VeDeyos* 1:4 end, 3:0.
57. *Kidushin* 31a.
58. *Shabbos* 10b.
59. *Berashis Rabbah* 1:1, Rashi on Genesis 1:1.
60. *Avos* 4:2; *Ohav Yisroel (Re'eh)* on Deuteronomy 8:16, *Shnei Luchos HaBris, Bais Chochmah* 1:22a, *Nefesh HaChaim* 1:12, *Avodas HaKodesh* 2:18, *Amud HaAvodah* (Chernowitz 5623) 101b.
61. *Nishmas Adam* #1 (Pieterkov, 5671) p. 16b.
62. *Avodah Zarah* 3a.
63. *Berachos* 8a. See *Nishmas Adam loc cit.*
64. *Baba Metzia* 59a, *Shaarey T'shuvah* (Rabenu Yonah) 3:141.
65. *Ikkarim* 4:33, *Nishmas Chaim* 1:13. See *Shaar HaGamul* p. 289.
66. See my article, "Immortality and the Soul," in *INTERCOM* 13:2, May, 1972, p. 6.
67. *Yerushalmi Arlah* 1:3 (6a), quoted in Rabenu Shimshon (Rash), *Tosfos Yom Tov*, on *Arlah* 1:5, *Tosfos, Kiddushin* 36b *"Kol Mitzvah,"* Turey Zahav, Yoreh Deah 294:25, and more specifically in this context in *Daas Tevunah* p. 5, *Pischey Chochmah VoDaas* #1, *Kinas HaShem Tzevakos* 5, KaLaCh Pischey Chochmah 4, *Avodas HaKodesh* (Chida) *Moreh BeEztbah* 319; *Nishmas Chaim* 2:6.
68. *Berachos* 6b.
69. *Betza* 32b. *Cf. Sh'mos Rabbah* 14:2.
70. *Avos DeRabbi Nathan* 31:1.
71. *Zohar* 1:4a.
72. *Yad, Tshuvah* 5:1, *Moreh Nevuchim* 3:17, *Emunos VeDeyos* 4:4 (64b), *Cf. Pirkey DeRabbi Eliezer* 15 (35a), *Menachos* 29b.
73. *Yad, Tshuvah* 5:4.
74. *Zohar* 1:23a, *Emunos VeDeyos* 3:0, *Reshis Chochmah* 3:1 (101b).
75. *Sotah* 14a.
76. See *Amud HaAvodah, Hakdamah Gedolah* #31; Rabbi Yitzchok Ashlag, *Hakdama LeSefer HaZohar* (in *Sulam*) #9, *idem., Talmud Eser Sefiros, Histaklus Penimis*, part 1, 1:4 (p. 15).
77. *Tanchuma, Kedoshim* 5, according to *Reshis Chochmah* 2:3 (59d).
78. *Menachos* 53b.
79. *Yad, Tshuvah* 5:1.
80. See *Gan Ravah* on Deuteronomy 7:10 (143b).
81. *Ikkarim* 2:11, *Akedas Yitzchok* 4 (36b), *Shiur Kumah* 18. *Cf. Berachos* 32a, *Bereshis Rabbah* 13:14.
82. *Kiddushin* 30a.
83. *Derech Mitzvosecha* (Chabad) *"Aroyos"* p. 29b f.
84. *Shavuos* 32a.

85. *Reshis Chochmah* 1:14 (41d).

86. *VaYikra Rabbah* 4:6.

87. *Sotah* 14a, *Yad, Deyos* 1:8. See above, note 75.

88. *Shabbos* 153b.

89. *Ibid.* 31a.

90. *Sifra ad loc., Yerushalmi Nedarim* 9:4 (30b), *Bereshis Rabbah* 24:8.

91. *Amud HaAvodah* 119a, 131a. Our sages thus teach us, "Love breaks all barriers," *cf. Bereshis Rabbah* 55:11.

92. *Amud HaAvodah* 136d.

93. *Nedarim* 64b. *Cf. Tikuney Zohar* 22 (66b).

94. *Berachos* 18b.

95. *Cf. Midrash Tehillim* 36:4, *Zohar* 1:23a, 2:184a, *Akedas Yitzchok* 70 (3:145b), *Etz Chaim, Shaar HaMelachim* 5, *Sefer Baal Shem Tov, Sh'mos* #9.

96. *Makos* 3:15 (23b).

97. *Cf. Emunos VeDeyos*, end of 4:1.

98. *Chulin* 60b.

99. *Zohar* 3:47b.

100. *Cf. Moreh Nevuchim* 3:26.

101. *KaLaCh Pischey Chochmah* #2.

102. *Zohar* 2:163a. *Cf. Baba Basra* 10a, Rabbi Yaakov Emden (Maharibatz) *ad loc.*

103. *Avos* 5:23.

104. *Tana DeBei Eliahu Zuta* 12 (17a).

105. *Tana DeBei Eliahu Rabbah* 16 (78a). Cf. *Menachos* 29b.

106. *Kuzari* 5:20 (48b), Ramban on Genesis 22:1, 22:12, Exodus 16:4, Deuteronomy 13:4, *Shaar HaGemul* p. 272, Radal on *Pirkey DeRabbi Eliezer* 31:2. See also *Bereshis Rabbah* 32:3, 34:2, 55:2.

107. *Sifri Ekev* 47, *Yalkut* 1:872.

108. *Sefer HaYashar* #1.

109. *Eruvin* 13b, according to *Avodas HaKodesh* 2:22, *Ikkarim* 4:29, *Cf. Yaaros Devash* 1:14, Bachya on Genesis 6:6.

110. *Sanhedrin* 24b.

111. Ibn Ezra *ad loc. Cf. Zohr* 2:89b.

112. *Derech HaShem* 1:3:4.

113. *Thirteen Principles of Faith*, #13; *Sanhedrin* 10:1. See *Bereshis Rabbah* 4:5.

114. This is the majority opinion, see *Emunos VeDeyos* 7:8, *Shaar HaGemul* p. 310, *Avodas HaKodesh* 2:41 f., *Shnei Luchos HaBris, Bais David* (30a f.), *Derech HaShem* 1:3:9, *Derech Mitzvosecha, Tzitzis* 14b. The Rambam, however, holds that the World to Come is for souls only, see *Yad, Tshuvah* 8:2, *Moreh Nevuchim* 2:27, *Igeres Techiyas HaMesim*. Also see *Kuzari* 1:114, 3:20,21, *Chovos HaLevavos* 4:4:6.

115. See *Moreh Nevuchim*, introduction to part 2, #16; *Amud HaAvodah, Vikuach Shoel U'Meshiv* #99.

116. *Cf. Shabbos* 89a, Bereshis Rabbah 48:11.
117. *Pischey Chochmah VoDaas* #3, *Shefa Tal* 3:1 (48a).
118. *Toldos Yaakov Yosef, VaYereh* 17a.
119. *Zohar* 1:4a.
120. *Bereshis Rabbah* 50:2, *Targum,* Rashi on Genesis 18:2, *Zohar* 1:127a.
121. *Pardes Rimonim* 6:6. See note 115.
122. *Amud HaAvodah* p. 83c.
123. *Sefer Chasidim* 530. *Cf. Zohar* 1:101b.